Philosophers in Perspective

There is an abundance now of books of 'readings' from the major philosophers, in which the selections are so often too brief and snippety to be of any great value to the student. There are also many collections of essays and articles about the major philosophers on the market. These too are unsatisfactory from the student's point of view in that they suffer severely from the defect of discontinuity and are unable to trace the scope and articulation of a man's work, as each contributor writes from the standpoint of his own interpretation.

There is a great need for books that are devoted to a single philosopher and that are written by a single author who is allowed the room to develop both his exposition and his examination of his subject in sufficient detail. *Philosophers in Perspective* satisfies this demand and makes available to students studies of all the major philosophers, and some of the undeservedly minor ones as well, which will afford them for the first time the opportunity of under-standing the philosopher, of coming to grips with his thought, and of seeing him in his place in the development of philosophy, or of his special area of it.

Each book in the series fits into this framework, but the authors are given the freedom to adapt it to their own requirements. Main emphasis will be placed on exposition and examination of the philosopher's thought, but enough will be written about the influences on him and about his own influence on subsequent thought, to show where he stands in the perspective of his subject. Wherever relevant, particular emphasis will be placed on the philosopher's con-tributions to moral and political thought, which have often in the past been treated cursorily as tailpieces to his writings on metaphysics and epistemology. This aspect of the series will prove most useful to students of politics, history and sociology.

See p. ii for list of titles in the series.

Philosophers in Perspective
General Editor: A. D. Woozley

Published titles
The French Enlightenment: J. H. Brumfitt
Rousseau: J. C. Hall
John Locke: J. D. Mabbott
John Stuart Mill: H. J. McCloskey
Kant: The Philosophy of Right: Jeffrie G. Murphy

Other titles are in preparation

THE FRENCH ENLIGHTENMENT

J. H. Brumfitt

**Professor of French
University of St Andrews**

Macmillan

2954

© J. H. Brumfitt 1972

First published 1972 by
THE MACMILLAN PRESS LTD
London and Basingstoke
Associated companies in New York Toronto
Dublin Melbourne Johannesburg and Madras

SBN 333 07576 5

Printed in Great Britain by
FLETCHER AND SON LTD, NORWICH

Contents

Preface

As my last chapter will show, there already exist many excellent studies of the French Enlightenment. The present book does not add anything significantly new to them, and what it has to say (apart from its errors) will already be known to the specialist. It seemed to me, however, as it did to the editors of this series of studies, that there was still a need for a short general survey of this important movement in the history of ideas, which would combine some account of the historical and social background with a closer look at the thought of the more outstanding individuals. This is what I have attempted to provide.

There are three significant questions which may be asked about the Enlightenment, as about any similar phenomenon: what? whence? and whither? I would have liked to deal with them all, but found it impossible to do so adequately in a book of this length. I have therefore sacrificed the 'whither?' and have not attempted more than the briefest discussion of the relationship of Enlightenment thought to the French Revolution, or of the reasons for its transmutation into (or replacement by) the complex of ideas and attitudes which we usually label 'Romanticism'. I have also dealt more briefly with the 'pre-revolutionary' generation of *philosophes* than with their predecessors. In the majority of cases, I do not regret this, for men like d'Holbach or Raynal do not appear to me to be profoundly original thinkers. It was with much greater reluctance that I decided to exclude any detailed consideration of Rousseau. It is true that the last thing Jean-Jacques would have wished would have been to be classed among the *philosophes*; it is true that one can advance many good reasons why he should not be. Yet in many ways he remains a man of the Enlighten-

7

ment, and the fact that in many others he transcends it, and can only be fully comprehended in the light of later developments, would not have led me to feel justified in omitting him, had I not known that he, alone among eighteenth-century French philosophers, was to have a companion volume in this series devoted exclusively to him.

I wish to record my thanks to the Leverhulme Trust for the award of a Research Fellowship and to the University of St Andrews for the grant of a period of study leave. Without this help, the book would have taken much longer to complete. Finally, I should like to express my gratitude to Professor A. D. Woozley and to my colleague, Dr S. S. B. Taylor, who read my manuscript with great care, and offered many helpful suggestions.

J. H. B.

St Andrews
May 1970

8

1 The Enlightenment

'I am', said Voltaire, 'like one of those little streams which are very clear because they are very shallow.' He spoke for himself, but something similar has often been said about the whole band of eighteenth-century French thinkers who appropriated to themselves the title of *les philosophes*, and who, for the most part, revered him as their leader. In the nineteenth century such a view was common; so much so, indeed, that the only definition of 'Enlightenment' given by the *Shorter Oxford English Dictionary* reads: 'Shallow and pretentious intellectualism, unreasonable contempt for authority and tradition, etc.; applied *esp.* to the spirit and aims of the French philosophers of the 18th c. 1865.' And if more modern writers are rarely so hostile, they are often suspiciously silent. The index of Russell's *History of Western Philosophy*, for example, does not contain the names of Diderot or Condillac. Isaiah Berlin's *The Age of Enlightenment* devotes well over two hundred pages to the British Enlightenment (mainly Locke, Berkeley and Hume), but barely a dozen to the French.

Is such hostility or neglect justified? From one point of view it can be. No eighteenth-century French thinker produced a philosophical system original or profound enough to stand comparison with those of, say, Descartes, Spinoza or Kant. Nor did any of the *philosophes*, criticise an existing system with the degree of penetration shown by Berkeley or Hume. If we are studying the history of philosophy with the aim of rethinking the thoughts of the men who have contributed most to it (in many ways an admirable procedure), we can educate ourselves tolerably well without ever making direct contact with the thought of any of the *philosophes*. The same would be true of the history of political thought were it not for one exception – Jean-Jacques Rousseau; and Rousseau, as his more nationalistic French critics like to remind us, was not, strictly speaking, a Frenchman, and would in any case object most indignantly to being classed with the *philosophes*.

However, there is another side to the coin. If we study the development of thought purely through the medium of the works of the greatest philosophers, we may sharpen our wits in the process, but we risk ending up with the same sort of distorted view as we would get if we studied history solely in terms of the activities of its Caesars, Cromwells and Napoleons. If we seek to understand how men in general have thought in the past or (what is perhaps more important) to be fully conscious of the origin and nature of the underlying assumptions which govern so much of the thought of our own society, we shall be interested in the dissemination of ideas and in their social relevance as much as in their originality. Viewed from this angle, the Enlightenment in general, and that of France in particular, presents a spectacle of absorbing interest.

Materially, mankind's progress during the last century and a half may have been unprecedented, but intellectually we are not so very far removed from the year 1800. Our universe is vastly larger than that of Laplace and contains many new and puzzling phenomena, but it is (at any rate to those of us who are not astrophysicists) recognisably the same place. Like Buffon, we inhabit an earth several million years old, and if we have filled in many of the gaps in its history, and in the history of the living beings which have evolved on its surface, we have done so partly by following the hints of a Maupertuis, a Diderot, a Voltaire or a Rousseau. We have, it is true, discovered a great deal that is new about the material universe and about ourselves, but we have done so, in the main, by following methods of scientific reasoning established by the end of the eighteenth century. Our social ideals, moreover, have changed even less. We all believe in (or, at any rate, we all pay lip-service to) liberty, equality, fraternity, democracy, tolerance, humanity. Our Declarations of Human Rights echo the concepts of the American Declaration of Independence or the French Declaration of the Rights of Man. We continue to have faith in progress, both material and moral, even though (and here we are by no means in conflict with the majority of eighteenth-century thinkers) we harbour grave doubts about the inevitability of such progress.

If the intellectual climate of the early nineteenth century is recognisably modern, that of the late seventeenth was still, in many ways, medieval. There were, of course, cracks in the Gothic edifice (there always had been), but it was still standing. Even in Protestant countries, but still more in Catholic ones, the Church had great temporal power which it employed (as men like Galileo found out to their cost) to suppress the dissemination of views in conflict with its dogmas. But the freedom of scientific inquiry was limited less by the actual physical power of the Church than by the intellectual power of the Christian tradition. Only a small minority sought to escape from the framework of Christian thought which was, indeed, both more coherent and more complete than any alternative they could escape to. If the Copernican revolution had thrown the heavens into some confusion (a confusion less disturbing at the time than some modern accounts have suggested), Christian order still prevailed in the sublunary sphere. How much this was so can be illustrated by the example of Descartes himself, who, as we shall see, started, in theory, with a slate wiped clean of all traditional knowledge, but soon found himself re-echoing the arguments of the medieval schoolmen and ended up trying to explain the Catholic doctrine of transubstantiation in terms of his particles of extended matter in motion. An even better illustration is provided by the case of Bossuet. Admittedly, Bossuet was the most influential spokesman of the French Church in the age of Louis XIV and hence had his feet firmly planted in the orthodox camp, but he was well aware of the scientific discoveries of his age and was very far from being an obscurantist. In his *Histoire universelle*, he could confidently describe a world which, as biblical

11

chronology proved, had been created some four thousand years before the coming of Christ, and interpret its subsequent history in terms of the working out of the designs of divine providence. In his *Politique tirée de l'écriture sainte*, he could prove, from the account of the Old Testament, that monarchy was a divine institution, and from the same source he could deduce all the qualities which it should exhibit. For Bossuet, as indeed for almost all his contemporaries, geological and biological evolution were as yet undreamed of; the theatre of human history was a small area of the Middle East and Europe and the most important events in that history were the Flood and the Incarnation; human nature, radically corrupt since Adam's sin, could never hope to make real progress in either knowledge or wisdom; in any case, man was much better employed seeking his spiritual salvation than in vain attempts to understand and control this world.

I have, of course, somewhat exaggerated the contrast between the two ages. There were, in the seventeenth century, men of science who tried to pursue their aims rationally and experimentally and who envisaged the possibility of mastering nature; there were those, such as Grotius, who sought to secularise the concepts of natural law and to lay the foundations of a code of international and social justice; there were exponents of democratic ideals, like the English Levellers (who, however, usually expounded them in 'religious' terms). Equally, there were men in the early nineteenth century, such as de Maistre or Bonald, compared to whom Bossuet was an enlightened liberal. Yet, by and large, it probably remains true that the average educated man's map of his intellectual universe was more completely redrawn in the eighteenth century than in any similar period before or since.

The men who did the redrawing constitute what we call the Enlightenment. It is, indeed, tempting to decide not to try to define the term more closely than this. For 'Enlightenment', like 'Renaissance' or 'Romanticism', is one of those terms which the historian of ideas is forced to use if he is to be anything but a mere compiler, but which, as he is well aware, cover an enormously complex field of intellectual and social phenomena which are often contradictory and which can certainly never be exhaustively listed. He is aware, too, that if he attempts to list them he is in danger of adopting the essentialist fallacy of giving his terms 'real' existence and of proceeding to fruitless discussions about whether Hume, say, or Rousseau, 'really belongs to' the Enlightenment. He rarely succeeds in avoiding these pitfalls entirely – nor, doubtless, shall I.

The Enlightenment had no fixed body of doctrine. It included atheists, deists, Protestants and Catholics; aristocrats, democrats and admirers of enlightened despotism; idealists and materialists, Cartesians and anti-Cartesians, retiring scholars and embattled propagandists, wise men and fools. Very few of its great figures are entirely typical of it. Nevertheless, considering that it spanned a century and a continent, it was a remarkably coherent and self-conscious phenomenon. Though the English word was only adopted later, its German original – *Aufklärung* – had already become a rallying-cry, and the French proclaimed their age to be 'le siècle des lumières'. Throughout Europe men united with the common purpose of 'enlightening' themselves and their fellows; and though they were far from agreed on all matters, they had enough in common to constitute a recognisable international movement.

In the first place, they rejected the authority of tradition in every sphere of knowledge. In this, as in other things too, they were to a large extent the heirs of Descartes, whose *Discours de la méthode* of 1637 contained one of the most influential and radical denunciations of hitherto accepted approaches to science and philosophy. If man was to find truth, then he must begin by scrapping all the alleged knowledge he had inherited from the past and return to first principles – to those clear and distinct perceptions which were so self-evident that they could not be doubted. Only thus could science be established. Authority, whether it be that of Aristotle, Galen or Cicero, or that of the general consensus of opinion, was deemed worthless. As for those branches of knowledge which, like history, appeared necessarily to repose on such authority, they were not worth wasting time on.

Authority, however, especially in seventeenth-century Europe, inevitably meant the authority of the Church, which extended over every aspect of intellectual inquiry. Though Descartes did his best (and a very good best it was) to avoid a clash between his principles and the dogmas of orthodox Christianity, such a clash was in the long run inevitable, and it was to constitute one of the main features of the struggle of the Enlightenment. It took various forms, for some of the Protestant Churches (and many individuals in the Catholic Church too) were prepared to move a long way in the direction of rational deism or 'reasonable' Christianity and hence to compromise with the spirit of the Enlightenment. This happened, for example, in Scotland, where many of the leading figures of the Enlightenment were themselves prominent churchmen. But in those Catholic countries where the Church was both intolerant and authoritarian, and where, into the bargain, its wealth excited the indignation and jealousy of its opponents, the conflict was to be a bitter one. Such was the case in France.

The rejection of authority would not, however, have resulted in any such conflict had it not been coupled with a positive believe in some alternative method of discovering truth. The absolute sceptic would probably have been prepared to keep his doubts to himself and would certainly not have risked persecution by proclaiming them. But the men of the Enlightenment were far from being absolute sceptics. They were convinced that they had a method of attaining truth: the method of scientific investigation. The principles of this method went back to Bacon and Galileo and, indeed, far beyond, but once again they had been formulated with exceptional clarity in Descartes's *Discours*. They were to be modified, as we shall see, in the course of the seventeenth century, and these modifications were to culminate in the work of Newton and Locke, who were to be the acknowledged masters of Enlightenment thought.

14

> Nature and Nature's laws were hid in night,
> God said: 'Let Newton be' and all was light,

proclaimed Pope, and he was far from being the only Englishman to lapse into verse on the subject. English, Dutch, Germans and (rather belatedly) French were united in seeing in Newton's *Principia Mathematica* of 1687 and, to a lesser extent, his *Opticks* of 1704, not only the fullest and clearest statement of the scientific, 'analytical' method (the 'geometric spirit', as it was later to be called), but also the proof that this method was capable of achieving a decisive breakthrough in the sphere of knowledge. A simple mathematical law had been discovered which explained phenomena as apparently diverse as the movement of the tides, the fall of an apple and the rotation of the planets. More modern critics see in Newton's work the culmination of seventeenth-century science rather than the beginning of a new epoch, and point out that, like Descartes, he did not fully succeed in eliminating the conflict between the 'rational' and the 'observational' elements of his thought. Yet for generations after his death, Newton seemed to have lit a beacon which would guide mankind to success in almost every field of inquiry, including many far removed from that of mathematical physics.

This would have surprised Newton, for he was far from imagining that he had created a method for the analysis of human psychology or the reform of civil society. This father of the Enlightenment was in many ways remote from the movement he engendered. First and foremost a mathematician and physicist, when he ventured beyond this sphere it was to indulge in relatively orthodox activities such as the computation of biblical chronologies. In this sense, he clearly belongs to the seventeenth rather than the eighteenth century. Locke, on the other hand, exhibits all the features of the change from one age to the next. Though no mathematician, he was a man of scientific interests (he had had a medical training) and an admirer of Newton, but he applied himself not to the physical sciences but to the study of man and society. In his most in-

15

fluential work, the *Essay concerning Human Understanding* of 1690, he imparted (or so, at any rate, it seemed to his more enthusiastic admirers) an almost Newtonian simplicity to the problems of the origin, nature and scope of human knowledge. Ideas could not be innate as Descartes – following the Platonic tradition – had asserted; they were, or they derived from (Locke is a little obscure here) sense impressions or introspection. All knowledge came from experience and, though Locke himself certainly never said so, it seemed to follow that understanding was itself derived from experience. What Locke appeared to have achieved was an explanation of human nature which did not need to have constant recourse to any theological doctrine. So much was this the case, that when he tentatively and briefly suggested (in the last Book of the *Essay*) that it was not impossible for God to give the power of thought to matter, he was immediately denounced for opening the door to materialistic atheism. This was in all probability not his intention, and the argument of the *Essay* is just as consistent with an idealist philosophy as it is with a materialist one. But Locke certainly appeared 'scientific' in a way that Descartes and his successors did not. He also appeared, though the conclusion was only consciously drawn at a much later date, 'democratic', since if men were formed by experience alone, they were all originally equal in ability and would, provided their experiences were the same, remain so.

Such a 'democratic' thesis was doubtless far from Locke's mind, but it is not inconsistent with other aspects of his thought, for political and religious liberalism were certainly dear to him. Together with his patron, the Earl of Shaftesbury, he had been involved in political plots to prevent the accession of the Catholic James II to the English throne, and his *Two Treatises of Civil Government* (which he published anonymously in 1690 and only acknowledged on his deathbed) were not, as has long been supposed, a justification of the Revolution of 1688 but rather, in origin at least, an incitement to it. The central ideas of this work – the criticism of absolutist theories, the assertion

16

of a social contract and of the right of a people to depose a monarch who broke it – were not new in the late seventeenth century. But coupled with the assertion of the natural sociability of man and a greater emphasis than heretofore on the rights of private property, they added up to a justification of constitutional government which made a powerful appeal to middle-class Europe and which was not to be seriously challenged until the advent of Rousseau.

Finally, in his *Letters concerning Toleration* (1689–90) and his *The Reasonableness of Christianity* (1695), Locke dealt with two other themes which were to be central to the Enlightenment. The urge to retain what was best in religious thought, whilst rejecting superstition, intolerance and dogma, characterised most, though not all, of its leading figures, and in their belief in the moral and social desirability of toleration they were even more united.

Locke, then, heralds the coming of the new age. Seventeenth-century science had forged a tool: the method of inquiry which had become known as the 'geometric spirit'. It had used this tool for the purposes for which it was most obviously adapted: the study of mathematics and the physical universe. If it had sought to change man's world, it had done so only in marginal ways (Descartes, for example, had hoped that his method would lead to great progress in the field of medicine). It was not interested in social problems and was most happy to adopt, as final rather than provisional, Descartes's 'provisional morality' of accepting existing political and social institutions. It would have liked to adopt a similar attitude to religion, though this sometimes proved more difficult, as the Church claimed authority over science too. Yet if its spirit was conservative, the implications of its method were revolutionary. The Enlightenment grasped this same tool – the geometric spirit – and proceeded to employ it in a radically different way. It aimed not merely to understand the world but also to change it. Traditional religious beliefs were to be examined in the light of reason and morality, and if they failed to pass the test, they were to be denounced as fraudulent or

17

harmful. Social institutions were to be subjected to similar scrutiny and, if necessary, to receive similar treatment. The scientific method was to be put to work for the material, but above all for the moral benefit of mankind.

To some extent, as we have seen, these were Locke's aims, but in the following century they were pursued with increasing assurance, with redoubled propagandist fervour, and with an ever-widening vision. To begin with, as is seen in the work of Bayle, the young Montesquieu, or the English deists, the emphasis was on negation: the myths which obscured men's view of society, of religion and of history were to be shown up for what they were. Later, the Enlightenment sought to contribute more positively to what Lessing called 'the education of the human race'. It is a roughly accurate approximation to say that the first half of the eighteenth century was predominantly destructive and the second half constructive. It was in this latter period that the French *philosophes* in particular tried to create their 'heavenly city': to devise the schemes and blueprints which could form the basis of material and moral progress. In doing so, it is true, they sometimes departed from the cautious spirit of inquiry to which, in theory, they were wedded. Yet such lapses, they would have argued, were excused by the overriding importance of the goal they had set themselves. When Kant suggested that the motto of the Enlightenment should be *sapere aude* – 'dare to know' – he gave expression to its first spirit. But when Voltaire said, 'I write in order to act,' he was perhaps expressing an even more important truth about the Enlightenment as a whole.

If this is so, then it is not enough to define the Enlightenment, as I have so far been doing, in terms of the development of its critical philosophical method. It is equally important to see it in terms of the society from which it sprang and which it sought to alter. It would never have preached its ideals with such propagandist fervour if it had not sensed the existence of an audience willing to receive them and potentially

18

numerous enough to put them into practice. Often, indeed, it would have been quite unable to do so. The greatest collective enterprise of enlightenment thought – the *Encyclopédie* of Diderot and d'Alembert – was also a major commercial enterprise which the publishers would never have promoted had they not been sure that even so expensive and voluminous a work would find a ready market. The Enlightenment reflected its age.

The age was a stable and a prosperous one. If wars continued to be fought, they were less devastating than those of the previous century and, in Western Europe at least, were mainly confined to frontier areas. If famine could still occur (as in France in 1709) and the plague could still strike (as in Provence a decade later), neither scourge produced the calamitous results known in earlier centuries. Civil strife had not ceased, but major religious civil wars were a thing of the past, and the Revolution of 1688 – from which one may conveniently, if somewhat arbitrarily, date the beginning of the Enlightenment in England – had been (in England itself) almost bloodless. Agricultural production, static, or even declining, in the seventeenth century, was to revive again in the eighteenth, and population was to begin to increase. Above all, the nations of Western Europe witnessed an unprecedented growth in their commercial prosperity. All these developments provided grounds for considering the possibility of social progress in a far more optimistic light than ever before.

Those who had contributed most to this advance, and who had benefited most from it, were the middle classes. In England, as a result of the Great Rebellion and the Revolution of 1688, they had gained a share of political power. Similar developments had taken place in Holland. In France, under the authoritarian rule of Louis XIV, they had at least supplanted the aristocracy as the principal agents of royal government. To describe the Enlightenment as essentially bourgeois has its dangers. The nineteenth-century concept of class struggle was foreign to eighteenth-century thought; in some countries, political and social reforms were to be

19

undertaken primarily by enlightened despots; in France, the aristocracy was to make an important contribution to the ferment of ideas which characterised the Regency and the period immediately preceding it. Yet it was in the countries where the middle classes were most numerous and most powerful – England, Holland, France and parts of Germany – that the Enlightenment first took root; it was, on balance, the bourgeois who contributed most to it (though in the case of France, this could be disputed); it was certainly, for the most part, middle-class ideals that it preached. Technological progress was dear to its heart. If the *Encyclopédie* is now mainly consulted for its 'subversive' views on religion and politics, it was primarily intended, as its sub-title made clear, to be a dictionary of sciences, arts and crafts. The English Royal Society, in its promotion of the study of astronomy and geographical exploration, never lost sight of the interests of the maritime trader. The most positive achievement of the reforming ministers of Charles III of Spain was the promotion of local societies dedicated to agricultural and economic reform.

The more abstract virtues extolled by the 'enlightened' also tended to be those of the middle class. The stoic heroism of an earlier age was out of date. Enthusiasm of any kind became an object of distrust in 'Augustan' England. The Christian concept of charity tended to give way to that of 'benevolence' (the term was coined by the abbé de Saint-Pierre) with its overtones of humanitarian paternalism. Tolerance, cosmopolitanism, hatred of war, the defence of economic and political freedom, all had a special appeal to the growing middle class. The merchant became a hero, as he was in Sedaine's play, *Le Philosophe sans le savoir*, or as he appeared to Voltaire, who, in his *Lettres sur les Anglais*, asked, with heavy irony, which was the more useful, 'a lord, powdered to the tip of the mode, who knows exactly at what o'clock the King rises and goes to bed ... or a merchant who enriches his country, dispatches orders from his counting-house to Surat and Grand Cairo, and who contributes to the felicity of the world'. And in the same work, admiring the religious toleration to be found in the Royal Exchange, Voltaire noted, with obvious approval, that the word 'infidel' was there reserved for the bankrupt.

To associate the ideals of the Enlightenment with those of the middle class is not, of course, to deny their independent validity. Still less is it to suggest that the men who propounded them were only concerned with their own interests. Their detestation of cruelty, intolerance or barbarous judicial tortures sprang from a deep sense of outrage, and in propagating their views they often risked, and sometimes suffered, persecution. It does, however, help to explain both the fundamental unity which is characteristic of the Enlightenment in Europe and, since social developments in different countries were uneven, some of the diversities which nevertheless remain.

The Enlightenment was essentially cosmopolitan; so much so that the very title of this book, *The French Enlightenment*, though convenient and concise, may be somewhat misleading in that it tends to import into the eighteenth century a modern concept of 'national' cultures which was largely foreign to it. Newtonianism knew no frontiers; Dutch physicists such as Boerhaave and 's Gravesande were among its earliest defenders, and the Frenchman Voltaire and the Italian Algarotti among its most effective popularisers. Locke, Montesquieu, Voltaire, Rousseau, all attained similar universal fame. National feelings existed, of course, and they may in part account for the early resistance to Newtonianism shown by many French scientists, or for the continued popularity of Leibniz and Wolff in Germany. Yet cultural internationalism was even more apparent. Vico never imagined he would get a sympathetic hearing in his native Naples, and appealed to the Dutch journals instead. When, in 1782, the French *Encyclopédie méthodique* suggested that European culture owed little to Spain, patriotic Spaniards were understandably angered. Yet the most effective reply to the *Encyclopédie*'s article did not come from one of them but from an Italian, Carlo Denina; and it took the form of a speech delivered in French before the Royal Academy of Prussia.

This cosmopolitanism was not a new phenomenon. It had existed in the philosophical world since the Renaissance, and indeed long before. In the eighteenth century, however, it became more outspoken and more widespread. The *philosophe* saw himself, like the Chinese hero of Goldsmith's novel, as a 'citizen of the world'. *'Homo sum; humani nil a me alienum puto'* ran one of his favourite Latin tags. He enthused over the wisdom of the Chinese, the simple nobility of the North American Indians, the sexual freedom of the Tahitians. Except for the Pyrenees (for nothing good could possibly come out of the lands of the Inquisition) there were no frontiers which his sympathies could not cross. It is true that he often took more with him in these spiritual journeyings than he brought back, for he was a 'Newtonian' cosmopolitan who believed that nature remained constant, and he tended to find evidence of eighteenth-century 'rational' principles in the most remote and unlikely places. When he travelled into the distant past, he could become even more confused; Voltaire, for example, spent a great deal of time denouncing Herodotus' account of ritual prostitution in ancient Babylon because he could not conceive of Parisian duchesses behaving in the same way. However, such blind spots, regrettable though they may have been, only served to intensify the *philosophe*'s belief in the universality of his own values.

In the narrower European context, moreover, material circumstances aided the spread of cosmopolitanism. To begin with, especially around the turn of the century, the intellectual life of the continent had, as its focal point, the most 'open' of all European nations. Holland offered a refuge to persecuted thinkers from many lands: Descartes, Locke and Bayle are merely the most famous of the many who profited from it. The Dutch publishing trade was the freest and most flourishing in the world, and without it many of the outstanding works of the Enlightenment would probably never have seen the light of day. Dutch journals, particularly those published in French by Protestant exiles such as Bayle, Le Clerc or Basnage, became the market-places and melting-pots of all that was new in European thought long before either England or France had anything to rival them. If we seldom speak of a Dutch Enlightenment, this is partly because Holland (after the death of Spinoza in 1677) did not itself produce any thinkers of the first magnitude, but it is still more because the innumerable lesser men it did produce (who contributed more than anyone to the diffusion of the thought of Descartes, Newton, Locke and many others) seemed European rather than Dutch figures.

This was partly because they thought and wrote in 'European' – or rather in one or both of the two languages which served as international media of communication: Latin and French. Latin had long been the universal language of scholarship, and still remained so, to some extent, in the early eighteenth century. It was, however, being rapidly replaced by French. At the same time, moreover, French was in process of becoming the language of diplomacy, the language of many European courts, in short, *the* language of civilised living. The linguistic nationalisms of the nineteenth century were still in their infancy, and Frederick the Great, and thousands like him, regarded French as infinitely superior to their native tongues. This gave cultured Europe a linguistic unity which later, despite improved means of communication, it was to lose.

The men of the Enlightenment made full use of these advantages for they were, in the main, great travellers. This was the age of the grand tour, an age when even war only partially restricted the comings and goings of those who wished to see the world for themselves. Many of the French *philosophes* – Montesquieu, Voltaire, Diderot, d'Holbach, for example – travelled extensively. Visitors to France were just as numerous – Englishmen like Bolingbroke or Gibbon. Scots like Hume or Adam Smith, Italians like Algarotti or Beccaria, Spaniards like Aranda or Olavide. The *salons* of Paris, and learned bodies such as the Royal Society, or the many academies which mushroomed throughout Europe, facilitated personal contacts. How extensive this intercourse was can be judged from the

23

endless stream of visitors from every country in Europe who made their pilgrimage to Ferney to visit the aged Voltaire.

All these factors contributed to the unity of the Enlightenment. Yet despite this cohesion, there was also much diversity. As social and cultural conditions varied in the different countries of Europe, so too did the temper of Enlightenment thought. The example of Britain illustrates this very clearly. Eighteenth-century England was a land of prosperity for all except those inarticulate farm-workers who were driven from their fields as a result of the enclosures. The middle classes had achieved some degree of political authority, especially after 1688, and the State was attentive to their economic interests. The established Church was relatively tolerant towards dissent, and showed some willingness to move in the direction of 'rational' theology (one of its leading spokesmen, Samuel Clarke, was also a distinguished disciple of Newton). Until the advent of the Hanoverians, however, this situation seemed far from secure, and the preceding quarter of a century – from Locke to, say, Collins – was a period of sharp intellectual conflict. As the threat of a Catholic Jacobite restoration receded, however, the English Enlightenment took on a more complacent look – best illustrated, perhaps, by Addison and Steele. Others, like Bolingbroke or Gibbon, were to be less complacent, yet there never developed any concerted movement akin to that of the French *philosophes*. Indeed, were it not for the ferment of the early years of the century, and the revival of political radicalism in its closing ones, one would be tempted to deny that there was ever any body of opinion which really merited the title of 'the English Enlightenment'.

Despite its political union with England, Scotland presents a very different picture. At the turn of the century the country was still economically backward, and torn by bitter religious strife. Only after the failure of the 1745 rebellion did the growth of commercial prosperity rapidly gain momentum. The Scottish Enlightenment, which took form about the same time, was a child of prosperity and stability. Like its English counterpart. it was characterised by moderation. It did not propose radical political reforms, nor did it come into serious conflict with the Church, for some of its adherents such as Robertson the historian, were themselves leading members of the Scottish Kirk and steered that institution into 'enlightened' paths. Yet it maintained a cohesion and a vigour without parallel in England, producing many men of the calibre of Ferguson, Robertson or Black, and, in Hume and Adam Smith, two figures of world stature. This unity and vitality may have owed something to Scottish national sentiment and to the fact that Scotland was far more open than England to continental, and particularly French, influence. It sprang too, no doubt, from the fact that the 'enlightened' Scots did not feel so secure as their compatriots south of the Border. They were aware of being outnumbered by the 'barbarian' clansmen of the north and the fanatical Calvinists in their midst. This insecurity acted as a constant challenge, and the result was an outburst of activity which placed this small nation on an intellectual level with the greatest in Europe.

In both these cases, however, the Enlightenment came, so to speak, from below. One example may serve to illustrate (though it does not necessarily typify) those in which it was largely imposed from above. Charles III of Spain came to the throne in 1759 and set about trying to reform the most backward and traditionalist country in Western Europe. Though a pious Catholic, he intended to be an enlightened despot, and this brought him into conflict both with the Inquisition, whose powers he succeeded in restricting, and with the Jesuits, who were finally expelled from the country. His main aims were social and economic reform, and to achieve them he gave executive power to a small group of administrators who did much to reverse the decline in population in the more stagnant areas, who pressed forward with agrarian and industrial reform, and who tried to modernise the educational system. Among them were men like Campomanes, Jovellanos and Olavide, who were influenced by enlightened ideas from France and Britain. Practical

25

men, though not original thinkers, they achieved much in a short space of time. Their disunity, however, together with the hesitations of the King, allowed the Inquisition to stage a come-back and, in a celebrated *autillo*, to condemn one of the most active and outspoken of them, Olavide, to imprisonment. This, followed by the outbreak of the French Revolution and later by the Napoleonic invasions, was to destroy much of what they had achieved. The Spanish Enlightenment proved a heroic failure.

Elsewhere in Europe (and not only there, for Olavide came from Peru, and the Declaration of Independence from the United States) the Enlightenment assumed different national forms. France was no exception. Yet in many ways France *was* exceptional. The most populous country in Europe (twenty million inhabitants as opposed to the six or seven of Britain or Spain), France had a prosperous middle class and an unsurpassed intellectual tradition. Yet she also possessed a powerful and intolerant Church, and a social organisation which, both in theory and in practice, was in many ways still feudal. Louis XIV had reigned despotically, but with the help of middle-class functionaries. The eighteenth century was to be an age of economic advance, but politically it was to witness the resurgence of the aristocracy. This situation, unparalleled elsewhere in Europe, was to produce an 'Enlightenment' which was both more complex and more radical than any other.

2 The Fortunes of Cartesianism

There are, then, two ways of looking at the origins of the Enlightenment: from the point of view of its method of investigation, or from that of the problems it found needed investigating and the conditions it felt needed changing. The philosophical chicken did not, of course, precede the social egg. It is nevertheless convenient to look at it first, for whereas we can pick up most of the threads of the French social situation by beginning in the 1680s, to understand the geometric spirit we need to go back, if only briefly, to Descartes.

Cartesianism, it is generally agreed, was (and possibly still is) a dominating force in French intellectual life. But just what was Cartesianism? To proclaim oneself a Cartesian might almost seem contradictory, for Descartes insisted that one should reject all intellectual authority and rely on one's own good sense (a quality he optimistically believed to be widespread); to be a good Cartesian, then, one should begin by throwing away the ladder Descartes himself had provided.

Many 'Cartesians' did just this; or at any rate they ignored, refuted or transformed a great deal of the master's teaching. Yet there was a central core which they, together with many who regarded themselves rather as anti-Cartesians, continued to accept. It is best formulated in the four principles which Descartes expounded in the *Discours de la méthode*:

The first was never to accept anything as true which I did not clearly know to be so: that is to say, carefully to avoid precipitation and prejudice and to include nothing more in my judgements than what presented itself so clearly and distinctly to my mind that I had no occasion to doubt it.

The second, to divide each of the difficulties which

27

I examined into as many parts as were possible and were necessary better to resolve them.

The third, to conduct my thoughts in an orderly way, beginning with the objects which were simplest and easiest to know, then climbing slowly, as if by steps, as far as the understanding of the most complex; supposing there to be an order even among those which did not naturally follow each other.

And the last, to make everywhere enumerations so complete and reviews so general that I might be certain I had omitted nothing.

Simplifying these principles, and stripping them of their mathematical overtones, we can describe Descartes's method as one of cautious and systematic inquiry aimed at the reductive analysis of complex phenomena into their simplest constituent parts, which can be explained in terms of truths which are self-evident; the parts are then reassembled in an equally systematic way, to explain the working of the whole. There was, of course, nothing completely new in any of these elements. What was relatively new was the coupling of a sceptical unwillingness to take anything on trust with the belief that common sense, clarity and systematic logical argument offered a key which would open vast new storehouses of knowledge.

This method became linked with the name of Descartes, not because he invented it, nor even because he formulated it with special clarity (on the contrary, it is, in some ways, far from clear), but because he appeared, with the help of it, to have solved many scientific problems and to have created an all-embracing philosophical system. However, closer inspection, in the seventeenth and early eighteenth centuries, was to reveal that there were aspects of, and problems in, that system which the method (even in the expanded form which Descartes gave it in the *Regulae*) did not deal with. It gradually became increasingly apparent that there were conflicts and even contradictions in Descartes's aims and methods, and the subsequent history of 'Cartesianism' is in large measure the story of attempts to resolve these.

To begin with, the method Descartes actually employed in his various investigations is by no means so simple as the four principles suggest. He started by making the distinction between spirit and matter more absolute than ever before and, discarding the qualitative, scholastic concepts (essences, virtues, accidents, etc.), asserted that the fundamental characteristic of matter was extension and its mode of existence (imparted to it by God) was motion. In this way, he created a new universe which could be observed, measured and quantified. In some works such as his *Dioptrique*, he showed, by a brilliant combination of observation, experiment and mathematical analysis, just what this method was capable of. But he was by no means always so consistent. Though he was not as hostile to the experimental method as many of his critics have suggested, he tended, as he himself later recognised, to neglect it in favour of more abstract forms of argument. Moreover, though he was undoubtedly a great mathematician, he could also neglect mathematics. In his *Principes*, for example, particularly in the third section where he puts forward his famous theory that the motion of the moon and the planets is to be explained in terms of vortices (*tourbillons*) of 'subtle matter', one looks in vain for the sort of mathematical formulations which were to characterise Newton's explanations of the same phenomena. Instead, one is presented with a series of diagrams in which innumerable tiny balls make interesting patterns. These diagrams *look* scientific, like those of the *Dioptrique*, but in fact they are not based on observation, being instead imaginative illustrations of how Descartes conceived the universe might work. Here we reach the third aspect of Descartes's method; the one Newton was attacking in his famous phrase '*hypotheses non fingo*'. Descartes explains the motion of the planets in terms of a 'common-sense' hypothesis: things do not move unless there is something to move them – hence the subtle matter; observation shows that vortices of such matter would cause larger bodies placed in them to orbit around their centre – hence it is reasonable to assume that this is what happens. Many of Descartes's

29

explanations of the mechanism of the human body were arrived at in a similar way and appeared equally 'reasonable'. Descartes's system was so persuasive, and came so near to explaining so much, that for some time, and by some people, it was accepted as a whole. However, the more discerning scientists, like Huyghens, realised that Descartes's hypotheses were far from being demonstrations. They could, moreover, be shown to be in conflict with the observed facts: bodies immersed in a whirlpool would not have behaved according to Kepler's laws of planetary motion; the human heart did not act as a furnace. In ways like this, the inadequacies of Descartes's method began to reveal themselves.

Other cracks in the structure of the system also became increasingly apparent. The rigid distinction which Descartes had made between spirit and matter was of benefit to the physical sciences in so far as they could thereby free themselves from problems they were ill-equipped to tackle. However, this was only the case if one ignored the soul, and Descartes himself had no intention of doing so. He attempted to reunite it with the body by suggesting the pineal gland as a rendezvous, but even he recognised the unsatisfactory nature of this hypothesis. The problem was left as an unwelcome legacy to his successors, and, as we shall see, they were to split in trying to solve it. There was, moreover, a more fundamental dichotomy in his thought, or rather, perhaps, in the psychological motivation behind it. In rejecting authority, and in proclaiming, sometimes with an almost mystical intensity, that science could lead man to mastery over nature, he seemed to epitomise a new and revolutionary spirit of confident rationalism. Yet in other ways he was much more conservative. His hypothesis of complete scepticism had quickly been followed by an assurance that he would continue to accept the traditional religious, moral and political beliefs of his own country. He made every effort to reconcile the tenets of his own philosophy with the doctrines of the Catholic Church, and though a concern for his own safety was not foreign to him, his religious beliefs were probably completely genuine. The possibility of conflict with religious, and still more with secular authority, was apparently made even more remote by the limits which he imposed on the field of scientific and philosophical inquiry. A smattering of historical knowledge was doubtless becoming to a man of culture, but more than this was a waste of time; the study of history could never be 'scientific', nor, by implication, could those of politics and society; Descartes therefore ignored them.

If these divergencies and contradictions are visibly in the thought of Descartes himself, it is hardly surprising that the subsequent history of Cartesianism made them even more manifest. Despite Pascal's shrewd criticisms of the 'spirit of geometry', despite the doubts of a Bossuet who, though an admirer, sensed a threat to the authority of the Church, despite the hostility of the Jesuits which resulted in the Sorbonne's imposition of a ban on the teaching of the new doctrines, Cartesianism spread rapidly in France. Many Jansenists (Pascal was an exception here) did not appear to find its optimism incompatible with their pessimistic theology, and the so-called *Logique de Port Royal*, an influential philosophical textbook published in 1662 by Arnauld and Nicole, was strongly influenced by Descartes's views. Though it was some time before the Sorbonne accepted it, Cartesian physics met with less opposition, and Rohault's *Traité de Physique*, of 1671, largely a restatement of the Cartesian position, rapidly became the standard work on the subject. By 1700, Cartesianism had almost become the official philosophy of France.

However, by this date it might be more accurate to speak of 'Cartesianisms' than Cartesianism, for Descartes's dualism was mirrored in the attitudes of his followers. Those who cultivated the natural sciences tended towards increasing experimentalism, influenced in part by Descartes's erstwhile opponent, Gassendi. They avoided the problem of the soul and its relationship to the body partly because it would have involved them in unwanted theological controversy, but also because, in some cases at any rate, they had become thoroughgoing materialists. This was probably

31

the position of Fontenelle and of many of the members of the circle which, in the early eighteenth century, formed around the duc de Noailles, and included notorious atheists like Boindin and Dumarsais. However, these Cartesian materialists did not publish their views in print, contenting themselves with circulating clandestine manuscripts. It was not until the appearance of La Mettrie's *L'Homme machine* in 1747 that a really thoroughgoing statement of the materialist position derived from Descartes was to see the light of day.

If 'scientific' Cartesians exhibited either a positivistic lack of concern with the problem of dualism, or moved towards a materialistic 'solution' of it, others were progressing in the opposite direction. They might be described as 'philosophical' Cartesians, for they took more interest than did the scientists in traditional philosophical questions such as epistemology. They were also predominantly theologians wishing to reconcile Cartesianism and Christianity. Their dissatisfaction with Descartes's explanation of the relationship between body and soul led them to deny that there could be a bridge between physical and mental phenomena and hence to a critique of the whole concept of causation, since if matter could not be 'known', its behaviour could hardly be explained. Geulincx was the first to work out what was later to be known as 'occasionalism', a theory which was to form the basis of the 'pre-established harmony' of Leibniz and Wolff: body and soul were like two clocks (one pointing to the time, the other striking the hours) which had been permanently synchronised by an act of divine will. However, the most influential of the 'idealist' Cartesians was the Oratorian priest Malebranche, whose *La Recherche de la vérité* appeared in 1674–5. Denying the possibility of direct knowledge of the physical world, Malebranche argued that the soul's contacts were not with matter but with God. Knowledge was knowledge of God, 'vision in God', but since Malebranche's God was a kind of rational essence of universal truth, this was all the knowledge of which man had any need. This may sound obscure (Locke considered Malebranche to have a positive genius for deliberate obscurity), but there were many who thought that Malebranche had achieved the reconciliation of Cartesianism and the Church. Up to a point he had, and this may account in part for the hostility which some of the *philosophes* (Voltaire, for example) showed towards Descartes: he had become identified with an authority they detested. Yet if we consider influence rather than intentions, we may well conclude that Malebranche's Cartesianism undermined rather than strengthened the position of the Church. Though his criticism of accepted ideas of causation was aimed at the materialists, it was to be one of the starting-points of Hume's atheistic scepticism; though his analysis of the role of imagination in thought may have had a similar purpose, it was to be used by men like Fontenelle to explain the origin of Christian myths; finally, his argument that miracles were incompatible with the nature of a rational, geometrically-minded God was to provide ammunition for many an eighteenth-century deist or atheist.

By the beginning of the eighteenth century, then, Cartesianism as a philosophical system, though superficially triumphant, was in reality falling apart. If Cartesianism remained a living force, as indeed it did, this was because its spirit of methodical inquiry had been applied in fields far removed from those envisaged by Descartes himself: to history, to ethics, to religion. Of course the movement of critical thought which characterised the turn of the century and which Paul Hazard christened *La Crise de la conscience européenne* was not wholly Cartesian. A current of scepticism, stemming from the Renaissance and passing via Montaigne and seventeenth-century *libertins* like La Mothe Le Vayer to a perspicacious critic of history and human nature like Saint-Evremond also played an important part. So too, though more indirectly, did the efforts of Catholic and Protestant to find historical justification for their respective viewpoints. Yet, as Cartesianism gave a new impetus to much of this questioning, and as many of the outstanding figures of the generation of crisis acknowledged their debt to Descartes, the movement may not unfairly be placed under his banner.

33

In one essential way, however, it was unlike the Cartesianism of Descartes himself: it was primarily negative, indeed destructive, in outlook, and it sought to destroy what Descartes had sought to preserve: the authority of orthodox Christianity, particularly that of the Roman Catholic Church. The discoveries of historians, chronologists, astronomers and geologists, coupled with biblical criticism of the type undertaken by Spinoza or Richard Simon, had made the traditional 'religious' view of man and his universe increasingly untenable. The power of the French Church, coupled with its ruthless suppression of 'heresy' – Protestant, Jansenist or sceptic – had destroyed much of the goodwill it might otherwise have continued to enjoy. The resulting conflict was to continue into the eighteenth century, but even before that it had produced, in Bayle and Fontenelle, the first great figures of the French Enlightenment.

Pierre Bayle (1647–1706) came from the south of France and was the son of a Huguenot minister. Like Rousseau or Gibbon in the following century, he became a youthful convert to Catholicism, and like them he soon repented. But the lot of a relapsed heretic was a hard one in seventeenth-century France, and Bayle had to flee to Geneva. He later taught at the Protestant Academy at Sedan, but when this was closed, as part of the gradual turning of the screw which preceded the repeal of the Edict of Nantes, he accepted a teaching post at Rotterdam. There he was to remain for the rest of his life, and there most of his works were written.

On the threshold of a new epoch, Bayle stands like Janus. In many ways he was the epitome of the seventeenth-century scholar: his learning was immense, but it was, for the most part, that of the humanist rather than the scientist; his argument, though it could be forceful and could exhibit a fine command of irony, had few of the qualities which appeal to the multitude. The intellectual dynamite of his ideas was often encased in quantities of protective wadding (as in the *Pensées sur la comète*), or buried deep in lengthy footnotes to lengthy texts (as in the *Dictionnaire*). Though, in the literal sense, he was a great journalist (his *Nou-*

velles de la république des lettres was a prototype of the scholarly periodical), he had few of the qualities, good and bad, which we tend to associate with the word, and which many of the *philosophes* were to exhibit.

Yet this apparently old-fashioned scholar was the source of many of the ideas which were to be dear to the eighteenth century, as well as of the facts which supported them. At times, indeed, he seemed to see deeper and farther than those that followed him. He had, for example, refuted eighteenth-century deism before it was invented. Even Voltaire, the most tireless exponent of this deism, could not but recognise the force of his criticisms, and one of the fruits of this recognition was to be the literary masterpiece of *Candide*.

Bayle was strongly influenced by Descartes, and many of his works can be seen as application of the spirit of Cartesian method to problems of history, philosophy and morality. Yet he was never a dogmatic Cartesian. In his early years he owed much to Montaigne and Gassendi, and later he was quite willing to reject the Cartesian concept of innate ideas in favour of the sensationalism of Locke. Moreover, though like Descartes he started from a position of complete scepticism and asserted that only in the combined light of reason and experience could one progress beyond this, he himself used this light to reveal errors rather than to illumine the path to new truths. At times, indeed, he seemed to destroy for the mere pleasure of destroying. Many of the articles of his *Dictionnaire* were devoted to the careful examination and refutation of obscure historical legends which hardly merited such treatment. His historical scepticism led him to assert that he no longer read historians in order to find out the facts (since this was impossible), but merely to discover what different interested parties *said* about the facts, and if he later modified this view slightly, it was only to the extent of conceding that one could be reasonably sure that such-and-such a battle had actually taken place.

Yet his destructiveness become far more purposeful when it was directed against 'living' myths – particu-

35

larly those associated with religion. The *Pensées sur la comète* of 1682 examined the popular myth (not quite so popular, by this date, as Bayle seems to imply) that comets were sent by God, either as a sign of his wrath (since they caused or presaged disasters) or to call men to repentance. With remorseless Cartesian logic, Bayle 'divided the difficulties into as many parts as were possible', and showed that each part was faulty. The authorities for the legend are poets and historians – a highly untrustworthy crew. All the evidence suggests that it is impossible for comets to be the physical cause of terrestrial disasters. There is no observable link between the appearance of comets and the outbreak of plagues, wars, etc., and hence no reason for supposing that the former presage the latter. To suggest that they are a call to repentance is absurd, for they are seen not merely by Christians but also by Muslims, pagans, etc. Could God wish to encourage them to practise their religions more zealously? At this point, Bayle begins to leave his comets behind and to embark on a discussion of the relationship between moral behaviour and religious belief. His conclusion, that there is no connection between the two, was not new, but had never before been so fully supported by argument. It undermined a fundamental belief of most Christians and indeed of many deists who, like Voltaire, believed in a 'policeman God'. It was to be hotly debated throughout the eighteenth century – as it still is, indeed, in the twentieth!

If there is no connection between human belief and human morality, there is none either between divine power and divine morality. The moral and physical evils which so manifestly affect the world make nonsense of the idea of an omnipotent and all-loving God. The heretical Manichaean view of a universe in which two equal principles of good and evil were locked in endless struggle seems far more in accord with the facts of life than does the orthodox view. Bayle emphasised this point at length in one of the footnotes (Remark D) to his article on Manichaeans in the *Dictionnaire*. He was to repeat it elsewhere; in the *Réponse aux questions d'un provincial*, for example: no human father, who had power to protect his children from harm, would allow them to suffer as God allowed man to suffer. The problem of theodicy, which Leibniz, and after him many more eighteenth-century thinkers, were to attempt to solve, was declared by Bayle to be insoluble if one followed the twin lights of reason and experience. Leibniz was only to 'solve' it by subordinating the latter to the former.

To most men in the eighteenth century – Christians as well as deists – religion and 'rational' religion were synonymous. It is therefore hardly surprising that Bayle came to be regarded as the great apostle of unbelief. His frequent affirmation of his faith was seen as a vehicle for irony or as a prudent precaution. The fideist position – that of accepting both reason and faith, whilst maintaining that the former can neither prove nor disprove the latter – was one which the age found difficult to comprehend. It may, nevertheless, have been the point of view to which Bayle genuinely subscribed, although interpreters of his thought are by no means in agreement on this question.

Be this as it may, Bayle's conviction that 'rational' religion was impossible led him, not surprisingly, to the conclusion that orthodoxy – any orthodoxy – was wrong. This belief was reinforced by the persecution he himself had suffered, and still more by that which descended on his Protestant fellow-countrymen after the Revocation of the Edict of Nantes. Bayle was to become a powerful critic of Catholic intolerance. His *Commentaire philosophique* of 1686 began with an examination of the biblical text which the persecutors quoted in self-justification. In one of his parables (Luke, ch. 14) Christ tells of the master who, when his invited guests failed to attend a feast, sent out his servant to bring in anyone he could, telling him: 'Go out onto the highways and hedges and constrain them to come in.' Bayle argued that to use this passage in defence of forcible conversion was not only arbitrary but monstrous, for belief was a matter of individual conscience and to try to force consciences was both absurd and barbarous. Yet even whilst denouncing the cruelties of Louis XIV, Bayle was also insisting, to the

37

discomfiture of some of his fellow-exiles, that Protestant orthodoxy was no better. He insisted, too, and this annoyed them even more, that the persecuted had no right to revolt. The *Avis aux réfugiés*, of 1690, which Bayle probably did not write, but which he certainly edited and approved of, called for moderation and respect for traditional authority at a time when Jurieu was invoking ideas of social contract and calling on the French Huguenots to revolt. Just as his plea for tolerance emphasised conscience rather than social utility, so too did Bayle's advice to the oppressed urge resignation, not social revolt. On both issues, the Enlightenment was, in the main, to take the opposite view. Nevertheless, his appeal for tolerance, at a time when France seemed to have forgotten the meaning of the word, was profoundly influential.

The *Avis aux réfugiés* was considered an act of treason by the more militant Huguenots, and as a result Bayle was dismissed from his teaching post. The remaining years of his life were devoted mainly to the *Dictionnaire historique et critique*, which was completed in 1697. Despite its bulk, despite the difficulty of consulting it (since many of the most interesting passages are in the least obvious places), despite the fact that it was soon to be banned in France, this vast compendium of historical, philosophical and religious doubts, demolitions and debunkings was to be the greatest literary success of the first half of the eighteenth century. For the *philosophes* in particular, it was an indispensable source-book, and for deist and atheist alike it became the bible of the struggle against orthodoxy.

Like Bayle, Bernard le Bovier de Fontenelle (1657–1757) had his roots deep in a seventeenth-century tradition, but a very different one. Born in Rouen, a nephew of Corneille, he first made a name for himself as poet and dramatist. His early work was marked by preciosity of both style and subject-matter, and a certain degree of affectation was to remain with him for a long time. However, he found that his literary gifts of clarity and lightness of touch could be used to ex-

38

pound more serious matters.

This was first made manifest in the *Entretiens sur la pluralité des mondes* of 1686. The setting is a conventional one of *salon* literature: moonlight shining on the gardens of the country château, whilst *la belle marquise* listens to the words of her admirer. The theme, however, is not love, but Copernican and Cartesian astronomy, which the speaker expounds with wit, simplicity and the occasional hint of *galanterie*. Moreover, though Fontenelle seeks to popularise astronomy, this is not his sole aim. The planets and stars are not just 'heavenly bodies', they have become *mondes*, and a good deal of the argument is devoted to showing that these countless worlds are in all probability inhabited like our own. Showing the caution which was to characterise him for the rest of his life, and provoke the scorn of more outspoken *philosophes* such as Voltaire, Fontenelle nowhere so much as hints at the conflict between such a view and the doctrines of the Church. The reader, however, could not fail to be aware of it. Indeed, the possibility of other planets peopled by intelligent beings raised endless difficulties for the orthodox (Would they have souls? Would they have incurred the guilt of original sin? etc.) and was probably far more disturbing to the anthropocentric assumptions of Christian thought than the 'Copernican revolution' itself. Fontenelle's relativism, expressed at times in striking images such as that of the roses, who assumed the gardener to be immutable and immortal, since none of them could remember him changing, let alone dying, undermined a host of accepted ideas.

The lesson was reinforced by Fontenelle's next important work, the *Histoire des oracles*. Christian tradition maintained that the oracles of pagan antiquity had been inspired by devils, and that they had all ceased with the coming of Christ. The tradition had recently been attacked in a lengthy Latin thesis by a Dutch scholar, Van Dale, and Fontenelle, duly acknowledging his debt, summarises and sharpens Van Dale's arguments. Like Bayle's *Pensées sur la comète* (which no doubt influenced it), the *Histoire des oracles* is an effective piece of 'Cartesian' historical criticism. Fontenelle examines the evidence for the tradition and shows how flimsy and unreliable it is. He proceeds to give a more plausible explanation based on human credulity and on the trickery of the priests, and to advance reasons why the early Christians should have been so anxious to believe in the supernatural inspiration of the oracles. However, the details of his arguments, on a subject of little direct interest to seventeenth-century readers, were less important than the general principles on which they were based, and in case the reader should fail to deduce these for himself, Fontenelle takes special care to emphasise them. The first, contained in his celebrated parable of the golden tooth (found, on examination, to be gold-plated, but only after the publication of several learned works 'explaining' it) was 'make sure of your facts before you try to explain their causes'. The second was to be mistrustful of all authority, but especially that of common consent: one witness against an existing belief was worth a hundred for it. Fontenelle combined a Cartesian faith in reason with an acute awareness (stemming from Saint-Evremond, Malebranche and Bayle) of how irrational men were. Passion, pride, self-interest and imagination had all contributed far more to men's beliefs than had reason.

Fontenelle was less of a scholar than Bayle, and his philosophical thought was not so deep or so wide-ranging. The 'facts' of the *Entretiens* were often rather inaccurately copied from not very reliable sources; those of the *Histoire des oracles* mostly came straight out of Van Dale. The problems of moral philosophy (of which theodicy may be considered an extension) did not particularly concern the younger man. Yet as propagandist and journalist he excelled, and in this way he is more akin to the *philosophes*. Brevity, clarity, concentration, topicality and wit all typify his writing. His *Digression sur les anciens et les modernes,* for example, was a brief but decisive intervention in a famous quarrel which up to then had generated more heat than light, and one of the first clear statements about the nature and the limitations of progress.

Above all, Fontenelle was a man of science. The works we have been discussing, and which contain most of his original contributions to the history of ideas, all belong to one short period of his life. He had, however, well over half a century left to him, and after 1690, when he was elected to the Academy, he largely abandoned his literary and historical interests, becoming instead the semi-official spokesman of scientific thought. In 1699 he was elected to the Academy of Sciences and later became its permanent secretary. Protected by the duc d'Orléans, he survived the inquisitorial regime of the last years of Louis XIV, though a Jesuit denunciation of the *Histoire des oracles* threatened him with persecution. Though his personal contribution to scientific discovery was small, his influence in guiding and popularising scientific thought was immense.

Fontenelle had witnessed the triumph of Cartesianism. He was also to witness its decline, for though its spirit survived in the *philosophes*, orthodox Cartesianism soon succumbed to pressure from the new doctrines of Newton and Locke. Cartesian cosmology, it is true, fought a strong rearguard action in France. This may have had something to do with national pride (Dutch Cartesians took much less convincing), but there was a more important reason. Descartes's vortices might not have fitted the observed facts, but they were based on the clear and distinct idea of propulsion. The Newtonian concept of attraction across empty space, on the other hand, was incomprehensible to common sense. To accept it, argued the Cartesians, was to return to the scholastic concept of 'occult qualities', and before one knew where one was one would be back with Molière's hypochondriac, affirming triumphantly that opium puts you to sleep because it has a 'dormitive virtue'. Newton, it is true, had foreseen this type of objection, and taken care to explain that he was describing mathematical relationships, not the essence of matter. Yet when, in the preface to the second edition of the *Principia*, Roger Cotes seemed to suggest that attraction was a quality of matter, Newton did not protest. It was, then, not unreasonable for the Car-

41

tesians to be suspicious.

Slowly, however, they gave way. When Newton died, in 1727, Fontenelle, who had long supported Descartes, spoke his praises before the Academy of Sciences and kept the balance between the two men almost steady. A few years later, having returned from England an enthusiastic, if not particularly well-informed, Newtonian, Voltaire expounded the new gospel in his widely read *Lettres philosophiques* (1734). His *Éléments de la philosophie de Newton*, of 1738, was a much more informed work. Meanwhile Maupertuis, also just back from England, published, in 1732, a far more authoritative defence of Newtonianism. It was Maupertuis, too, who later provided one of the most important pieces of experimental verification for Newtonianism, when his expedition to the Arctic demonstrated that the earth was flattened at the poles (a 'Cartesian' earth would have been elongated). By the time d'Alembert wrote his masterly survey of the development of scientific thought for the Preliminary Discourse of the *Encyclopédie* (1751), Newtonianism appeared to have won the day.

Locke, meanwhile, had triumphed more easily. This was not altogether surprising, for whereas, in cosmology at least, Newton seemed to be in direct conflict with Descartes, Locke's analysis of human understanding tended to ignore the Cartesian problem of the relationship of mind to matter, and to deal instead with what happened to 'ideas' within the mind. It is true that Locke attacked the concept of innate ideas, but some orthodox Cartesians, like Régis, had already moved some way towards a similar position. What opposition there was in France came mainly from the disciples of Malebranche. Malebranche, however, belonged to a religious order with Jansenist sympathies, and this may help to explain why the Jesuits, who remained hostile to Descartes, accepted Locke with alacrity. True, Locke's hypothesis about thinking matter continued to give some cause for alarm, especially when it was highlighted, as it was in Voltaire's *Lettres philosophiques*. Yet Lockean sensationalism was to be widely accepted in France until, in the second half of

42

the century, its 'dangers' suddenly came to be realised.

The 'defeat' of Cartesianism was real, and the spirit of the Enlightenment was to be both more observational and more experimental. Yet the change was not so complete as some of the victors imagined. The philosophies of Newton and Locke were Cartesianism with a difference rather than something totally new. Like Cartesianism, they both rested on a compromise between the rationalistic assumption that the universe had 'meaning' and a purely empirical approach. Moreover, the type of Cartesian hypothesis which Newton refused to 'feign' was still to play its part in the thought of men like Montesquieu or Condillac. Cartesianism had been absorbed rather than rejected.

3 The Breakdown of Absolutism

Ideas may generate their own momentum, but only within certain limits. It may be argued that much of the early eighteenth-century 'crisis of conscience' was an almost inevitable result of the seventeenth-century scientific revolution. Yet it would never have developed its distinctive anti-Christian tone if the Church had not been, in some sense, a political as well as an intellectual force. Still less would it have developed a critique of political society, if that society had not itself manifested its inadequacy.

After the anarchy of the religious wars of the sixteenth century, France experienced a period of slow consolidation, in which the most decisive part was played by Richelieu. Though in practice he exercised something of a personal dictatorship, the Cardinal's avowed aim was to restore the power of the monarchy. This he did by destroying the political and military independence of the Protestants, by strengthening the central administration through the creation of royal *intendants* to rule the hitherto semi-autonomous provinces and by suppressing the more powerful and turbulent aristocrats. Marzarin, who succeeded him, adopted similar policies, but met with more resistance. The civil wars of the Fronde, which lasted, with intermissions, from 1648 to 1653, began as a middle-class revolt against increased taxation, but were gradually transformed into a last attempt by the more powerful nobles to assert their independence. Weakened politically by its lack of united aims, and morally by the cynical self-interest manifest in many of its leaders, the revolt was finally defeated, more by Mazarin's diplomatic skill than by military measures. With it perished, for a time at least, the ideals that had inspired it. The French middle classes had not produced a Cromwell,

44

or the organisation to back him, and for a long time ceased even to dream of political power. The aristocracy realised the impossibility of a return to feudalism. Disillusioned with revolt, the country was ready to accept royal authority. When, after Mazarin's death in 1661, Louis XIV took power into his own hands, it found a monarch capable of providing it.

Louis took over many of the policies of Richelieu and Mazarin, but he applied them both more swiftly and with greater success. His success had many causes: the attraction of the monarchical ideal and of the personality of the young king himself; the improved economic situation resulting from a relatively long period of European peace; his ability to choose able men such as Colbert and Louvois as his subordinates. Though Louis could be ruthless (as he was, for example, towards his disgraced finance minister, Fouquet), there was a new atmosphere of freedom and prosperity in the country as a whole as well as new gaiety and splendour at court. The first two decades of the new reign were a period of industrial and commercial revival, of legal and administrative reform, of the reconstruction of Paris, of Molière, Racine and Lully; in short, the period of which most French historians are really thinking when they refer to the seventeenth century as *le grand siècle*. Political opposition was largely neutralised. If the wealthier nobility were increasingly deprived of power, they were compensated with lavish pensions and with splendid, if largely decorative, roles in the increasingly elaborate ritual of the court. If the *Parlements* – the accepted, if unrepresentative, voice of middle-class opinion – were soon denied their traditional right of remonstrance, the middle classes themselves were enjoying economic prosperity and were further encouraged by the spectacle of the high offices of state being filled by men drawn from their own ranks. Both Protestants and *libertins* enjoyed a fair degree of freedom, for Louis, seconded in this by Colbert and, to a lesser extent, Louvois, was no friend of the *dévot* extremists of the Counter-Reformation.

During these years, political theory had kept in step with practice. St Paul's dictum that all power was or-

45

dained by God, which for centuries had served as the starting-point for Christian discussion on the nature and limits of secular authority, provided the foundation for the doctrine of the divine right of kings, even though it could equally well be applied to justify any other existing form of government. However, the Catholic Church had always been careful to remind monarchs not only of their religious duties but also of the distinction between absolute power and arbitrary power. The monarch was, or should be, wedded to the interests of his subjects and bound by the precepts of natural law; to that extent, he was a constitutional monarch even though this 'constitution' was both unwritten and unenforceable. These limitations, vague though they were, were not to the liking of seventeenth-century autocrats and their supporters, and though they were not directly attacked, they were nevertheless to some extent undermined, both in France and in Protestant countries, by the expression of more uncompromising absolutist principles. In 1625, for example, shortly after Richelieu's rise to power, the French clergy declared that kings were themselves gods. One of Richelieu's protégés, Pierre de Marca, in his *De Concordia* of 1641, sought to prove that secular and spiritual power had an identical divine origin, and, though this extreme view was condemned in Rome, he received an archbishopric from the Cardinal. The extreme absolutist viewpoint was also defended by Jesuits like Le Moyne and by Protestants like Merlat, whose *Traité du pouvoir absolu des souverains* appeared, ironically enough, at the very moment when Louis was using his absolute power to destroy the Huguenots. It was reinforced, too, by the development of the Machiavellian idea of *raison d'état* in a number of works, like those of Naudé and Rohan, published during the period of Richelieu's 'rule': the interests of the state (which in practice meant those of the ruler) were to be regarded as paramount, and if they conflicted with ideas of equity, so much the worse for the latter.

The Fronde brought a temporary reaction, and some of the *parlementaires* sought justification for their revolt in the contractual theories of their English counterparts. More consistent opposition to the extreme absolutist view came from the Church, and more particularly from those who feared that the French monarchy might be tempted to emulate Henry VIII of England and assume complete control of ecclesiastical affairs. However, this threat, though it seemed real enough at the height of Louis XIV's early quarrels with the Papacy, soon evaporated. Compromise proved possible, and it was to be epitomised by the work which may be considered the most authoritative statement of the political theory of the age of Louis XIV: Bossuet's *Politique tirée de l'écriture sainte*. Bossuet argued that monarchy was both the most natural and the most efficient form of government; above all, Bible in hand, he demonstrated how God had ordained it for his chosen people. Yet he was equally aware of the temptations and dangers which beset the monarch, and his work is not so much a eulogy of the monarchical ideal as a constant warning to kings that they should not only fear God but should, in all their doings, be *'soumis à la raison'*. Whilst denying the right of any human agency to limit the power of the sovereign, Bossuet is in fact insisting that any 'just' monarch must impose limitations on himself.

Bossuet's *Politique* was only published posthumously, in 1709, and by this time its argument had a somewhat hollow ring, for Louis XIV's reign was ending in tyranny, famine and defeat. The early years of the 'sun king' had approximated much more closely to Bossuet's ideal. It is true that they never quite possessed the degree of peaceful symmetry their admirers have seen in them. The mercantilist economic policies of the peace-loving Colbert paved the way for the wars with Holland, and subsequently with the rest of Europe, as much as did the bellicose ambitions of Louvois or of Louis XIV himself. The wars of the seventies did much to destroy the economic achievements of the years of peace, and the growth of the influence of the devout and intolerant Mme de Maintenon in the late seventies, the permanent removal of the court from Paris to Versailles in 1682 and the death of Colbert in 1683 were all significant steps in the gradual alienation of

47

Louis from the interests and the affections of his people. Yet the majority, dazzled as they were by the splendours of the reign, were scarcely aware of this change in the situation, and the more perceptive minority chose to keep silent, or (as happened particularly in the case of the Protestants) to go into exile. Open expression of concern at the way things were developing was almost non-existent.

This state of affairs was profoundly modified by the repeal of the Edict of Nantes in 1685 and by the persecution of the Huguenots which accompanied it. The Protestants who fled to Holland, England and Switzerland provided the nucleus of an opposition. In some ways it was a powerful nucleus: it possessed, in the free and flourishing presses of Holland and England, an unrivalled medium for the propagation of its views; it included men of the calibre of Bayle and Jurieu, of Pierre Coste, soon to undertake the task of translating Locke, and of Rapin de Thoyras, who, early in the following century, was to write what may be described as the first great Whig History of England. Yet it also suffered from a certain lack of unity. Some, like Bayle, advocated complete toleration and opposed armed resistance. Others, like Jurieu, in his *Lettres pastorales*, strove to maintain a Protestant orthodoxy and, combining sixteenth-century French Protestant doctrines with seventeenth-century English ones, proclaimed the existence of a social contract and the right of an oppressed people to overthrow the monarch who had broken it.

The gradual tightening-up of the censorship and the merciless hunting down of Protestant ministers who returned to France limited the extent to which the ideas of the exiles could penetrate the homeland. Moreover, as France soon found herself at war with Holland and other Protestant countries, it was easy, and to some extent legitimate, to condemn the Huguenots as enemy agents. This, coupled with the fact that their appeal was directed primarily to their fellow-Protestants, meant that the exiles made little or no direct impression on the Catholic majority. However, as conditions changed within France itself, those who in 1685 would not have dreamed of listening to Protestants arguments

48

began to change their minds. In addition, new forms of internal opposition developed.

Catholic opinion was almost unanimous in welcoming the repeal of the Edict of Nantes. However, the subsequent Huguenot exodus – particularly the flight of tradesmen and skilled artisans from the south – rapidly led some discerning minds to have second thoughts. The extent of the economic damage which it caused may have been exaggerated by later apostles of tolerance, but it was certainly significant enough to lead Vauban, in his *Mémoire pour le rappel des Huguenots* of 1689, to draw up a list of the losses sustained and to urge, on purely opportunistic grounds, the recall of the exiles. On a more idealistic plane, similar views were soon advanced by leading churchmen such as Fénelon, to whom the forcing of consciences became as repugnant as it was to Bayle.

The repeal of the Edict of Nantes has often been regarded as the symbolic first step on the road which led to the abolition of the French monarchy just over a century later. Yet other factors were probably more important. In 1686 war broke out again and it was to last, with only brief intermissions, until Louis XIV's death in 1715. It was to be accompanied by economic decline, by a considerable fall in population, by famine, by the introduction of new forms of penal taxation, by the increasingly harsh suppression of all manifestations of political dissent, above all (in the War of the Spanish Succession) by military disasters; had the British not withdrawn from the war and made a separate peace in 1713, these might well have resulted in the dismemberment of France. The French monarchy never fully recovered from them – especially as far as financial stability was concerned – and it is in them that we must seek the sources of many of the political positions of the French Enlightenment.

Whilst Louis XIV lived, open political opposition was impossible. 'The great subjects,' said La Bruyère (and by this he meant primarily religion and politics), 'are forbidden.' However, there were ways of circumventing this prohibition, and La Bruyère himself found one of them. His *Caractères*, first published in

1688 and later added to, were a literary masterpiece and one of the bestsellers of the age. In part, no doubt, their success resulted from the fact that the 'characters' portrayed could very often be identified. In addition, however, he was a social critic of no mean stature and reflected the growing disillusionment of his age. It is true that he avoided the 'great subjects', or rather that he proclaimed himself (sincerely, no doubt) a fervent monarchist and a devout Catholic. However, the ideal monarch whom he described in a section of his work was in some ways remarkably unlike Louis XIV. Master of irony that he was, La Bruyère was probably well aware of this. More important, he portrayed a society riddled with the corruptions of greed and power. Nobility had lost its original meaning and had become a marketable commodity (as was indeed increasingly the case as Louis sought new means of financing his wars); the new 'aristocrats', moreover, were often the most ruthless and unscrupulous of men. Even the old nobility had nothing great about them but their names. Authority could be monstrously abused, as it was by the administrator who casually signed an order which starved a whole province and whom La Bruyère ironically excuses on the grounds that he was suffering from the after-effects of a good dinner. '*Je veux être peuple*,' La Bruyère proclaimed, and in some ways his most sympathetic portrait is the celebrated one he draws of the sufferings of the peasantry – wild animals reduced to the barest level of subsistence, but who, nevertheless 'sont des hommes'. Yet he was not 'peuple'. A tutor in a princely household (and the Condé family itself could have provided material enough for several books), he was in a unique position to observe society, but remained an isolated figure – a *déclassé* in the modern sense of the term. Generously 'revolutionary' in many of his sentiments, he was often narrowly conservative in his opinions, and in his estrangement from the society around him he foreshadows the great *solitaire* of the following century – Jean-Jacques Rousseau.

Open social criticism, even written from such a conservative standpoint, became increasingly rare as the despotism of Louis's last years tightened its grip, though there were some notable exceptions such as Lesage's play, *Turcaret*, a harsh satire on financiers, performed with considerable success in 1709. For the most part, however, the opposition had to express itself in allegory, to publish anonymously or clandestinely, or to circulate its ideas in manuscript or by word of mouth. Despite these limitations, the voice of protest increasingly made itself heard.

Among the disguised attacks on royal despotism may be reckoned what some would regard as the greatest of all French tragedies – Racine's *Athalie*. The parallels between Athalie's persecution of the Jews and Louis's persecution of Racine's fellow-Jansenists were obvious, and it was difficult not to see a contemporary message in the denunciations of the corruption of power. But *Athalie*, which first appeared in 1691, was never performed publicly until after Louis's death, and so had little immediate influence. The most effective allegorical attack came from Fénelon, whose *Télémaque* – written originally for the instruction of the heir to the throne – was published clandestinely in 1699 and was to become one of the bestsellers of the eighteenth century. The didactic content of this novel describing the wanderings of the son of Ulysses probably accounts for its failure to captivate the modern reader, but the description of the city of Salente, where the interests of the people predominated over those of the rulers, where the law was mightier than the lawgiver, where aggressive war and ostentatious luxury were abhorred – a city which was clearly the antithesis of the France of Louis XIV – made a powerful appeal to eighteenth-century hearts.

Télémaque was the most famous, though far from the most outspoken, French example of a literary genre which became the most popular vehicle for radical social criticism in the late seventeenth and early eighteenth centuries: Denis Vairasse's *Histoire des Sévarambes* is more typical. The 'extraordinary voyage', as it is usually called, normally had a contemporary setting and its heroes were transported to exotic and fantastic lands akin, in some ways, to those visited by the best-known English 'extraordinary voyager',

Gulliver. However, whereas Swift's aim was predominantly satirical, the French writers were more concerned with describing Utopias from which the evils they saw around them had been eliminated. Among these evils, the power of the priests (a consequence of all revealed religion) rated high, and the newly discovered lands were often havens of the purest deism. But they were political paradises too: lands of agricultural plenty and enlightened urban planning, of peace and tolerance and of communistic egalitarianism. Though they were too remote from reality to offer practical programmes of political reform, their success testifies to the general dissatisfaction with things as they were, and their influence on later more down-to-earth reformers, though difficult to demonstrate, may well have been considerable.

Less numerous, but more immediately important, were the more direct protests and projects of reform which, for the most part, were published anonymously. In the background, of course, were the radical political writings of the past, culminating, perhaps, in Spinoza's *Tractatus* of 1670 – perhaps the most devastating onslaught on religious and political authority to come out of the seventeenth century. Yet though he was much read, Spinoza was not always understood and was in any case regarded as too 'dangerous' to be acknowledged, still less followed. In any case his views were not to the taste of the more articulate of the reformers of the late seventeenth and early eighteenth centuries who were neither radical critics, nor, like the authors of imaginary voyages, utopian dreamers: their criticisms were for the most part practical, and their dreams, when they had any, evoked idealised images of the bygone days of feudalism. This is hardly surprising for they belonged, in the main, to the aristocracy. It was with the second estate rather than the third that positive criticism of the social and economic developments of the late seventeenth century originated, and they were to continue, in the following decades, their theoretical and practical opposition to what they regarded as royal despotism. In doing so, they were to appeal to the older traditions of French society and to stress, not unnaturally, the preponderant role which the nobility had had in them. Historians of the Revolution, and of the period immediately preceding it, have often dealt harshly with men who appeared to them the entrenched defenders of privilege, and in the context of the second half of the eighteenth century they may well be justified in their criticisms. Yet just as 1789 could never have happened without the 'aristocratic' revolution which preceded it, the political and social doctrines of the French Enlightenment – even though, taken as a whole, they can still meaningfully be described as 'bourgeois' – were the product of aristocratic discontent as much as of the aspirations of the 'rising' middle classes. It would of course be naïve to assume that the dissident aristocrats were disinterested in the views they advanced; but it is also naïve – though somewhat more common – to assume the exact opposite. Their efforts to recover their privileges were not divorced from a general concern for the welfare of the State, and in defending their own liberties, and seeking a theoretical justification for them, they upheld the cause of liberty in general and widened men's understanding of the nature of political society. They wore their feudalism with a difference, and it is no accident that the greatest of them – Montesquieu – can be considered both as the founder of modern sociology and (though the description would not have pleased him) as one of the most distinguished exponents of a basically feudal ideal.

It was not until well into the eighteenth century, when the traditional hostility between *noblesse d'épée* and *noblesse de robe* had largely disappeared and when the *Parlements* had come to provide a new focus of discontent, that the aristocracy became an organised opposition, and even then many aristocrats – among them great ministers such as Machault or Turgot – remained wedded to the ideal of a reforming monarchy. In the seventeenth century, the belief that the King could be persuaded to adopt new policies still prevailed, as it did, for example, with Vauban. Vauban came from relatively impoverished noble stock and had made his name as Louis XIV's great master of siege

53

warfare before turning his attention to the economic and social ills of his day. His reaction to these was, like La Bruyère's, basically conservative. A devout Catholic, he was shocked at the growth of irreligion, particularly among younger army officers who should, he argued, be dismissed (unfortunately they were too numerous to punish!). A believer in the traditional role of the nobility, he deplored its continued dilution through misalliances and the sale of offices; in particular he urged the preservation of the privileges of the ancient *noblesse d'épée* and thought that high rank, especially in the army, should be reserved for its members. Yet he was both a practical man and a humanitarian and these qualities gave him a new open-mindedness on many matters. Devout he may have been, but he was one of the first to realise the evil effects of the repeal of the Edict of Nantes and to demand the recall of the Huguenots. Moreover, he combined piety with strong opposition to the temporal power of the Church and that of religious orders. 'France will never recover its ancient splendour except by destroying monasticism and breaking with Rome, not by alterations in religion,' he remarked, and his hostility to the monks, visible also in his criticisms of their role in the colonies, was largely motivated by economic considerations. Similarly, despite his belief in aristocratic traditions, he was willing to allow the poorer nobility to engage in trade without permanent loss of status. Such views were to be re-echoed by many of the *philosophes*.

In the last decades of his life, Vauban wrote many *mémoires* and projects, most of which never saw the light of day. He was, however, unwilling to see his project for tax reform suffer the same fate, for he had worked on it for nearly ten years. He therefore risked publishing – though anonymously and clandestinely – the *Projet d'un dîme royale*. It appeared in 1707 and was almost immediately condemned by the King's Council. Action might very possibly have been taken against the author, too, but he was already a sick man and he survived the condemnation by only a few days. The *Projet d'un dîme royale* itself, however, lived to become an important influence on eighteenth-century social and economic theorists – particularly the physiocrats. Vauban urged that the existing tax system should be almost entirely abolished (he retained taxes on luxuries and a modified form of the *gabelle*, or salt tax) and replaced by two taxes – on the 'fruits of the earth' and on revenue from property, profits and wages. The rates at which these taxes were levied were to be variable, but they were to constitute the essence of the *dîme royale*. Such a plan might have gone far towards solving the financial problems which beset the monarchy during the greater part of the eighteenth century, but in the closing years of the War of the Spanish Succession, when finance was on a hand-to-mouth basis. it was not really practical politics. Yet Vauban's work made a powerful impact, and the sweeping nature of the reforms it proposed aroused more enthusiasm than did the somewhat more cautious suggestions along the same lines made, a few years earlier, by Boisguillebert in his *Détail de la France*. The names of the two men have often been linked, partly because of the publication of an edition of Boisguillebert's work under Vauban's name. But Boisguillebert was critical of Vauban's ideas, and in reality their views were sharply opposed, especially on more fundamental matters of economic theory. Though Vauban's emphasis on agricultural produce makes him in some ways a predecessor of the physiocrats, he was basically still a mercantilist. Boisguillebert, in his criticisms of the effects of Colbert's policies, showed himself a far more profound economic thinker. If the eighteenth century did him less than justice, this was partly, no doubt, because propagandists found the military genius turned social reformer the more congenial figurehead for their cause.

Fénelon, probably the most important figure in the aristocratic opposition to the despotism of Louis XIV, was also to be transformed by propagandists, such as his disciple Ramsay and, later, Voltaire, into a hero, or even a martyr, of the pre-Enlightenment. The transformation was not a difficult one, for there was much in Fénelon's personality, career and opinions to make it credible. The young abbé who had been made tutor to

55

Louis XIV's grandson and later appointed to the arch-bishopric of Cambrai seemed destined to worldly suc-cess. Yet he compromised his future by his opposition to the persecution of the Huguenots and still more by his espousal of the heretical doctrine of quietism, which led to a long battle with the orthodox Bossuet, to his defeat and subsequent dignified retraction, and to his exile to his archbishopric. Quietism was no doubt poles removed from eighteenth-century deism, but the two certainly shared a tendency to reject, or at any rate to by-pass, certain aspects of institutionalised religion, and it was therefore possible for something of the spirit of Fénelon to pass into that of Rousseau's *vicaire savoyard*. Fénelon, moreover, had other and deeper affinities with what is usually thought of (not altogether correctly) as the 'Rousseauist' side of the eighteenth-century mind. His *Télémaque* (the one work which everyone knew) blended Homeric charm and political moralising with a good deal of what the later eighteenth century was to know as *sensibilité* – touching and tearful scenes of recognition and repen-tance. The archbishop sympathised with human mis-fortune – particularly, it often seemed, that of the lowly. Before the abbé de Saint-Pierre had coined the word *bienfaisance*, he seemed to be the epitome of it.

His political career, like his religious one, had a cer-tain tragic attraction about it. His influence over the heir to the throne was a profound one, and he could hope that when the young duc de Bourgogne suc-ceeded the aged Louis XIV, he would attain some measure of power, or at least see some of his ideas put into practice. But his hopes were ruined by the death of the duke in 1712, and he himself was also to die before Louis.

Finally, his political ideas themselves contained much to appeal to the *philosophes*. Many of them were easily deducible from *Télémaque*, but when, later in the century, his *Lettre au roi* was discovered and pub-lished by d'Alembert, they were seen in even clearer form. The letter was probably written in 1694, though whether it ever reached its addressee has never been finally established. Its criticism was uncompromising:

For about thirty years, now, your principal ministers have been undermining and overthrowing all the ancient maxims of the State to increase to the utmost your authority which had become theirs because it was in their hands.... You have been praised to the skies for having, or so it was said, eclipsed the greatness of all your predecessors put together, that is to say, for having impoverished the whole of France in order to introduce at Court a monstrous and incurable luxury.... They have been harsh, proud, unjust, violent, dishonest. Their only rule, both for the internal administration of the State and for foreign negotiations, has been to threaten, to crush, to destroy everything which resisted them.

After giving numerous examples of the aggressiveness and bad faith of Louis's foreign policy, Fénelon turned to home affairs:

Meanwhile your peoples, whom you ought to love as your children and who, up till now, have been so passionately attached to you, are dying of hunger. Agriculture is almost abandoned; town and country are denuded of their population; all forms of trade are languishing and no longer feed their workers. All commerce is destroyed. As a result you have destroyed half the real strength of your State to make and defend vain conquests abroad.

There followed a warning of growing disaffection: 'Your victories and your conquests no longer delight [the people]. The fires of sedition are slowly being lit everywhere.' Finally, abandoning the pretence of laying all the blame on the ministers, Fénelon attacked the conscience of the King himself:

You do not love God; you only fear him with the fear of a slave; it is hell you are afraid of, not God. Your religion consists merely of superstitions, of little superficial practices.... You only love your glory and your comfort. You relate everything to yourself as if you were the God of the world, and all

57

the rest had been created merely to be sacrificed to you.

If this letter did reach the King it may well have been one of the causes of Fénelon's exile. At Cambrai he had time to devote himself to the writing of *Télémaque*. But if he was henceforth cut off from the seat of power, his political activity increased again as the economic and military situation worsened during the War of the Spanish Succession. He became the central figure of a party which formed around the young duc de Bourgogne and had a number of highly titled adherents both within and outside the Government – among them the dukes of Chevreuse and Beauvillier. Together with the former, at a dark moment in the war, late in 1711, he drew up the *Plans de Gouvernement* to be proposed to the duc de Bourgogne.

These plans reveal the more positive aspects of Fénelon's political thought. They include much which would again have appealed to the *philosophes*: an overriding desire for peace, a determination never again to be involved in war with the rest of Europe; demands for vast reductions in court expenditure; proposals for the decentralisation of power and for the recall of the States General (which had not met for a century); limitation of the temporal power of the Church; greater freedom of trade, and many similar measures. Yet at the same time they illustrate the extent to which Fénelon, and the group around him, wished to put the clock back rather than forward. The starving populace he had pitied in the *Lettre au roi* was largely forgotten and even trade and commerce were relegated to the end of the plan. The role of the Church and the nobility were his main concern. His religious politics, on the whole, were ultramontane, and, though he could criticise Rome, he believed that Gallican separatism had gone too far. Though he opposed the forcing of consciences, he wished to destroy heresy within the Church and his plan to 'uproot' Jansenism was even more ruthless than the one subsequently employed. The nobility was to be purged of its recent, more doubtful additions, and misalliances were to be prohibited. Major offices in the royal household, in the army and in the Church were to be reserved for members of ancient noble families. It was primarily to the nobility that Fénelon looked for the regeneration of society.

Fénelon and his friends constituted the most powerful and the most positive of the opposition groups in the last years of Louis's reign. But there were others, too. The duc d'Orléans was a focus of one of them, particularly after the death of the duc de Bourgogne, when it became clear that Orléans would become Regent. The *libertin* Société du Temple flourished under the patronage of the Vendôme family – dissolute, distrusted, but never wholly disgraced – and though it did not meddle in politics it nurtured the greatest of the sceptics – Voltaire. The duc de Noailles, soldier and statesman, was another powerful patron of religious and political heterodoxy, and among those close to him was Henri de Boulainvilliers, deist and disciple of Spinoza, but also the most 'philosophical' of the protagonists of feudalism. As Louis approached his end, all these groups disseminated their ideas, and the more powerful and practical of them jockeyed for position, as did also Louis's illegitimate and much-favoured son, the duc du Maine (ably seconded by the duchess), and many more. In these struggles, as in those between the peerage and the rest of the nobility and between the *noblesse de robe* and the *noblesse d'épée*, political principle often played little part, as can be seen from the writings of their most notable chronicler, the duc de Saint-Simon, for whom questions of ceremonial precedence were often far more important than more substantial issues. Most of the ideas of the Regency already existed at this time, as indeed did most of its art forms, not to mention the less atractive sides of its pleasure-seeking mentality. But Louis kept the lid firmly clamped down on them, and it was not until after his death that the practicality of the new feudalism could at last be put to the test.

Louis XIV's funeral cortège carefully avoided Paris, but
there they were dancing in the streets. The icy grip of
despotism was ended and the thaw had arrived at last.
The rejoicing which followed was not altogether mis-
placed, but unfortunately it was overdone. The ice was
to return, even though it was never again to be quite so
thick.

Louis had done his best to ensure that his policies
should continue after his death. Mistrusting Philippe
d'Orléans, whom he regarded, rightly, as both de-
bauched and irreligious, he had tried to restrict his
powers as Regent. With the help of the *Parlements*,
Philippe succeeded in having these restrictions
removed. Mme de Maintenon, who had inspired many
of Louis's repressive policies, and Le Tellier, his much-
hated Jesuit confessor, were sent packing. There was
talk of recalling the Protestants, of summoning the
States General. Meanwhile, censorship was lifted, the
centralised bureaucracy dismantled and the Jansenist
quarrel appeased. Government was to be in the hands
of a series of councils drawn from the distinguished
members of the nobility, each of which was to have
wide powers in its own particular field.

Yet if Louis's deliberate precautions had been unsuccessful, he had nevertheless left behind him a legacy
of problems which the Regent, despite his good intentions, was to find insoluble. For over forty years the
aristocracy had been largely without political power
and the ineffectiveness of government by councils
showed that they had forgotten how to use it. The
Regent, threatened by many opponents, particularly
Philip V of Spain (who, by birth, stood nearer the
French throne), needed ministers who could act vigorously. Increasingly, he came to rely on his former tutor,

the future Cardinal Dubois. He also needed a remedy for the disastrous financial situation, and when efforts to make the war-profiteers disgorge proved largely ineffective, he turned instead to the financial wizard John Law. Law's 'system' led to a frenzy of speculation, followed, in 1720, by a financial crash which aroused popular resentment and brought the *Parlements* into open opposition. The Jansenist dispute, a further legacy of Louis's intolerance, also flared up again. The Regent had at first succeeded in stifling discussion of the Papal Bull *Unigenitus* which condemned many of the Jansenist and Gallican views expressed by the Oratorian Quesnel and which was highly unpopular with the *Parlements*, with the body of the clergy, and probably with the majority of the population. But Dubois, largely, perhaps, in order to obtain his cardinal's hat, pressed successfully for the acceptance of the Bull. The resulting battles between Church and *Parlements* were to last throughout most of the century. Jansenism (or what was called Jansenism, for it had now become remote from the austere theological doctrine of its founder) was probably the most important form of opposition to Louis XIV and his successors, and, on the level of myth and popular fanaticism rather than of rational thought, had at least as powerful an influence on the course of events as the new political and philosophical theories.

Faced with increasing opposition from almost every side, Philippe d'Orléans concentrated on defending his own position. The reformist schemes of his early years were largely abandoned. Intelligent and liberal though he was, the Regent was not the sort of man to court martyrdom in any cause. Dubois became increasingly powerful, and though he had contributed indirectly to the introduction of liberal ideas into France through the establishment of the English alliance, his later reconciliation with Rome led him increasingly to the defence of orthodoxy. Voltaire's epic poem, *La Henriade*, had praised an earlier English alliance, that of Henri IV with Elizabeth, and the work had had the Regent's approval. But it had also criticised the power of Rome, and when Voltaire sought to publish the

61

work in France, Dubois refused permission. This was but one straw in the wind, but when, in 1723, Dubois and Philippe died within a few months of each other, the hopes the Regency had raised had already largely evaporated.

Government by deliberative councils, rather than by secretaries of state and their dependent bureaucracy, had been one of the decentralising measures proposed in the group around the duc de Bourgogne. By 1715, however, the most eminent members of this group were all dead; happily so, perhaps, for as deeply religious men they would have been horrified to see power in the hands of a notorious *libertin* like the Regent. Fénelon, indeed, had almost been prepared to believe the popular rumour that Philippe d'Orléans had poisoned the duc de Bourgogne and others in the line of succession. However, Saint-Simon, who became one of the principal advisers of the Regent when he first came to power, had had close links with some members of the duc de Bourgogne's circle (though not with Fénelon himself) and it was probably he who was largely responsible for the introduction of the new system. Yet the name with which it is always associated is that of the abbé de Saint-Pierre.

When, in 1718, Saint-Pierre published his *Discours sur la Polysynodie*, he was defending, as he was well aware, a system which had already largely broken down. Though he did not say so explicitly, his work was written, in part at any rate, in an attempt to put right the defects of the system as it existed. He attributed the system to the duc de Bourgogne, yet his attachment to it may have resulted from the fact that he himself had put forward similar ideas (if the dating on the manuscript can be trusted) as early as 1702.

Despite a fair degree of naïvety and a great deal of enthusiastic long-windedness, Saint-Pierre was a thinker of considerable originality. His contemporaries and immediate successors often tended to regard him as an *esprit chimérique*, but his principal biographer, Drouet, describes him as an *esprit positif et terre-à-terre*. Both descriptions contain some measure of truth: his idealism could occasionally be 'starry-eyed'.

but the problems he dealt with, from systems of taxation (here he was largely a disciple of Vauban) to those
of keeping fit (he invented a sort of therapeutic rocking-
chair), were essentially practical. Noble himself, he
reflects in general the point of view of the aristocracy,
but at times he diverges from it markedly.

Saint-Pierre's most influential works were the *Polysynodie* itself (together with later clarifications of some
of its points) and the *Projet de paix perpétuelle*, first
published in 1713 and then, in an expanded form, in
1717. The *Projet*, which appeared just as a disastrous
European war was coming to an end, did not claim to
be entirely original, for Saint-Pierre admitted that
similar proposals had been made over a century before
by Henri IV and Sully. Yet in fact these had had
French advantage very much in mind, and Saint-
Pierre's work was much more genuinely international
in spirit. It proposed a general alliance of European
sovereigns to stabilise existing frontiers and then settle
all further disputes by arbitration. A Council of
Europe was to be created with powers to coerce those
who broke these arguments and with the right (given
the unanimous consent of member governments) to
make further common 'European' laws. If, as Voltaire,
Rousseau and others were to point out, the scheme was
impracticable in a Europe which contained so many
eighteenth-century 'Machiavellian' despots, it was one
of the most important manifestations of the cosmopolitanism of the age, and not without influence – partly
via Kant – on more modern peace-keeping organisa-
tions. Moreover, though hardly 'democratic' (since it
was based on a pact between existing sovereigns, and
thus 'froze' existing despotisms), it would, in fact, have
limited the sovereignty of these despotisms by imposing on them the general will for peace of European
peoples as a whole and so contained at any rate the
seed of the idea of popular sovereignty.

The *Polysynodie* was not really democratic either.
Saint-Pierre defended government by aristocratic
councils as the only practical alternative to the monarchical and ministerial despotism of Louis XIV. Of the
latter he was so openly critical that he was expelled
63

from the Academy as a result. Yet if Saint-Pierre thought the aristocracy were born to rule (he distrusted the idea of recalling the States General and disliked the mixed government of England), he nevertheless insisted that it should rule well, and here again one senses an unspoken appeal to some sort of popular sanction. The Regency councils had been chosen by the Regent himself, and Philippe d'Orléans had been anxious both to reward his friends and to include (and thereby neutralise) some of his opponents. Saint-Pierre, however, demanded that they should be elected, though without indicating precisely how, or by whom. Later, however, he tried to fill in this gap in his theory by proposing the creation of a 'Political Academy' – a small group of ninety *étudiants politiques* who would be trained as administrators: from them three candidates would be chosen for each important office, and the final choice would lie with the King. Members of the councils, too, would come from their ranks. The *étudiants* would be drawn from the magistracy, the nobility and the clergy. This meant that they would be predominantly of noble origin, but when coupled, as it was, with an attack on hereditary nobility and particularly on the dukes, this plan (an ancestor, perhaps, of more modern ideas of 'technocracy') was far removed from the traditional aristocratic thesis.

Saint-Pierre was not alone in giving this thesis a new look. It was also to be transformed, as well as deepened, by one of its most lucid and passionate exponents: Henri de Boulainvilliers. A member – probably the most influential one – of the duc de Noailles's circle, Boulainvilliers combined Spinozist deism with a belief in astrology, and a general attachment to aristocratic privileges with a surprising hostility to some of them. His influence before and during the Regency was already considerable, for many of his works circulated in manuscript and he counted men like d'Argenson among his close associates. But it was only after his death in 1722 that his writings began to be published.

Boulainvilliers's principal contribution to the aristocratic cause was to formulate its case in historical terms. This had been done before, particularly in the sixteenth century, but in the late seventeenth and early eighteenth, partly, no doubt, as a result of the growth of historical scepticism, such arguments had become relatively rare. In his *Histoire de l'ancien gouvernement de la France*, (published in 1727) and in a number of other works, Boulainvilliers brought them back into favour. For a time, indeed, they were to become the dominant form in which the fundamental political debate found expression. Eighteenth-century thought, and that of the *philosophes* in particular, has often been accused of being anti-historical, of drawing up blueprints of the future which rashly ignored the traditions of the past. Yet such attitudes, though they existed, were far from universal, as can be seen from the intensity of the debate which Boulainvilliers's work initiated.

French society, he argued, had come into existence as a result of the Frankish conquest of Gaul, and it was thus 'natural' for this society to continue to develop according to the traditions of political life then established. Not only was it 'natural', it was also 'right'. The Frankish conquerors, who had met in their *champs de mars* to deliberate on their policies and to choose (or, in some cases, depose) their monarchs, were free men, and feudalism as they had established it was the guarantee of liberty and consequently 'le chef-d'œuvre de l'esprit humain'. Alas, this happy state of affairs (happy, at any rate, for the conquerors) had not lasted. The rise of hereditary monarchy and the attempts of successive monarchs, and above all of Louis XIV, to impose centralised despotic control had diverted the course of French history from the paths which were 'natural' and 'right'. The nobility had lost its role and its privileges, and the peasantry (whose well-being, ideally at any rate, was the concern of the lord) had suffered too. The only ones to gain were a small section of the more powerful aristocrats (Boulainvilliers was no friend of the dukes) and the officers who had imposed the King's authority (he was no friend of the *noblesse de robe* or the *intendants* either). The way forward for France was the way back: to a decentralisation of power which would restore noble initiative and, with it, liberty.

Boulainvilliers belonged to the *noblesse d'épée*, and his views clearly mirrored this fact. But the *noblesse de robe* could and did put forward similar arguments. Throughout the crises of the Regency and later, in the thirties, when Fleury was to attempt to impose royal authority, particularly in religious disputes, they had fought for their right of remonstrance, seeing themselves as the true representatives of the nation as a whole. In 1732, when the struggles with Fleury were at their height, an anonymous pamphlet was published entitled *Judicium Francorum*. This pamphlet claimed that the *Parlements* – particularly the *Parlement* of Paris – were the inheritors of the traditions of the Frankish assemblies and the rightful representatives of the three estates of the nation. It echoed arguments put forward during the Fronde, and based its case on a long series of historical examples. The *Parlement* deemed it necessary to condemn the work, but it probably had the secret approval of many *parlementaires*.

Boulainvilliers had despised the *gens de robe*, who in the past had often been the obedient servants of royal policies, and who had the reputation of being parvenu legalistic pedants. In the early years of the century, many of the *noblesse d'épée* would have agreed. But by the thirties, the *parlementaires* were clearly no friends to the King, and they had become increasingly recognised as 'receivable' in the highest society. The hostility between the two groups of nobles gradually diminished, and more and more the *Parlements* assumed the leadership of the aristocratic struggle.

The so-called *thèse nobiliaire* – the belief that life, liberty and the pursuit of happiness were best ensured by the existence of strong *Parlements* and a strong nobility as a bulwark against royal despotism – grew in strength, and was to find its most distinguished exponent in Montesquieu. The opposing view, the *thèse royale* which affirmed that the aristocracy were essentially concerned with the preservation of their own privileges and that necessary social changes could only be brought about by a centralised reforming royal government, also had its distinguished adherents. It was not, however, until the War of the Austrian Succession had made financial problems more acute that the opposition between these two *thèses* became clearly manifest in terms of actual policies. Moreover, useful though the distinction is, it has the disadvantage of suggesting a far greater degree of political polarisation than really existed in the minds of most men on both sides. Voltaire, for example, though usually in the 'royal' camp, was ready to take the other side when occasion seemed to demand it. Boulainvilliers's friend, the marquis d'Argenson, shared his opposition to despotism and his attachment to decentralisation, yet in his *Considérations sur le gouvernement*, written and circulated in the thirties, though not published till later, he showed himself hostile to the privileges of nobility and *Parlements* and asserted the need for a strong monarchy to bring about necessary financial and administrative reforms. However, his own experiences as a minister (and more particularly, perhaps, his dismissal) were later to change his views, and in the fifties he was even to talk of the need for a 'revolution' to diminish royal power.

In one field at least, though, the *thèse nobiliaire* received a direct answer. Boulainvilliers's interpretation of the Frankish conquests was refuted by the abbé Dubos's *Histoire critique de l'établissement de la monarchie française dans les Gaules* of 1734. That Dubos's work was politically motivated there can be no doubt, but it was not ostensibly so, and was all the more effective for that. Dubos asserted that the conquest of Gaul by a 'democratic' Frankish nobility had never taken place. If the Franks had met on their *champs de mars*, this was to discuss military tactics rather than political constitutions. If they had obtained power in Gaul, this was not the result of a 'conquest', but of an invitation from the Roman authorities of the province to the King of the Franks. Clovis and his successors were consequently the rightful heirs of the Roman emperors. As for the characteristic institutions of feudalism, these had only emerged centuries later.

The debate, despite the fact that Montesquieu,

though with reservations, supported the 'germanist' thesis, went, on the whole, in favour of Dubos and the 'romanist' interpretation, and modern scholarship tends to confirm this judgement. More acute minds (Voltaire's, for example) saw the futility of all this political antiquarianism, though this did not stop Mably, in his *Observations sur l'histoire de France* of 1765, rewriting the whole story from a 'popular democratic' point of view.

Mably's work, however, belongs to a much later period. During the first half of the century there was very little sign of any popular or middle-class opposition to parallel the highly articulate one of the aristocracy. The middle-class lawyers who have left memoirs lent their support to the *Parlements*, but tended to be more concerned with religious than political issues. This was also true of the most striking outburst of popular discontent – the manuscript *Testament* written some time in the twenties by an obscure parish priest, Jean Meslier. Meslier appears to have been the first to voice what was later to become quite a popular desire to see the last noble strangled with the bowels of the last priest. But his denunciation of despotism, though outspoken, was not original, and his utopian communism was, as we have seen, paralleled in the work of many creators of imaginary voyages. In any case, his work did not become known until Voltaire and d'Holbach published it much later in the century.

There was one work, however, which did express distinctively bourgeois criticism of the structure of French society. It did so with brevity and clarity, and its great success, despite official attempts to suppress it which included its burning by the public hangman, makes it a landmark in eighteenth-century thought. This work was Voltaire's *Lettres philosophiques* or *Lettres sur les Anglais*, published in England in 1733 and in France the following year.

Voltaire had been born plain François-Marie Arouet, the son of a successful notary. When, after the success of his first play, *Oedipe*, in 1718, he began to achieve literary fame, he thought it expedient to add the aristocratic-sounding 'de Voltaire' to his name. His wit soon led him from one aristocratic château to the next, and if it also landed him in the Bastille for a spell, the satirical lines on the Regent which were the immediate occasion for this sojourn do not appear to have had any deep political motive. Though he was certainly interested in history and in 'current affairs', and though work on *La Henriade* and friendship with Bolingbroke and other Englishmen had already made him something of an anglophile, he could not really be described as politically committed, though his strongly deist and anti-Christian sentiments were an open secret. Then, early in 1726, came the fateful beating which, after a quarrel with their master, he received from the servants of the chevalier de Rohan-Chabot, a member of a distinguished aristocratic family. His protests and threats of revenge led a somewhat embarrassed Government to send him once again to the Bastille and thence into exile. The place of exile – England – was, however, his own choice. When he returned to France three years later, he came home with a mind well stocked with English religious, philosophical and scientific ideas – even with an admiration for Shakespeare. Above all, however, he brought back his sense of grievance – against Rohan, against the Government which had imprisoned and exiled him, and, more generally, against the whole structure of the society which allowed such things to happen. He brought back, too, memories of a country in which things were ordered better, together with some of the political theories which prevailed there. This knowledge and these sentiments, coupled with the talents of a literary journalist of the highest order, brought forth the *Lettres philosophiques*.

Voltaire was a poet by profession and a deist by conviction, and not surprisingly literature and religion occupy far more space in his description of English life than do political and economic questions. In fact, only three of the twenty-five letters are devoted to these. However, the twin themes of liberty and class-equality are constantly cropping up elsewhere: in the description of the sturdy independence of the Quakers, for example, or in the accounts of the ways in which English society, unlike its French counterpart, has honoured scientists like Newton, actresses like Mrs Oldfield or writers like Matthew Prior. Voltaire's work is a splendid presentation of the values and achievements of English civilisation, even if he is somewhat over-lavish in his use of whitewash. Still more, it is an indictment of the social institutions of eighteenth-century France. Voltaire does not indicate precisely *how* the desired reforms in his own country are to be brought about (though the reader is left with the strong impression that he is by no means hostile to an 'English revolutionary' solution), but he illustrates very clearly *what* he wants done, and there is probably no more succinct formulation of the essential grievances of the French middle classes until the Revolution itself. The *Lettres* were, to quote Lanson's famous phrase, 'the first bomb to be thrown at the Old Regime'.

Three chapters, 'On the Parliament', 'On the Government' and 'On Trade', constitute the main explosive charge of this bomb. The first of these opens by quoting a phrase, used in parliamentary debate, of one of Walpole's main adversaries, William Shippen: 'The majesty of the people of England would be wounded....' Laughter, says Voltaire, greeted these words, but when they were emphatically repeated the laughter was silenced. No doubt, many French readers reacted in a similar way. There followed a parallel between England and republican Rome in which, after adroitly side-stepping the charges of corruption which were frequently (and rightly) levelled against the English Parliament, Voltaire makes the point that the aim of the English civil wars was liberty:

The English are the only people upon earth who have been able to prescribe limits to the power of kings by resisting them; and who, by a series of struggles, have at last established that wise government, where the Prince is all-powerful to do good, and at the same time is restrained from committing evil; where the nobles are great without insolence, though there are no vassals; and where the people share in the government without confusion.

70

The parallel with Rome soon gives place to a much more important one with France. The French civil wars of the sixteenth century, and still more the Fronde of the seventeenth, produced nothing but cruelty and bloodshed. The English civil war of the seventeenth century had 'a wise and prudent liberty for [its] object'. The execution of Charles I is partly justified by the reflection that he, had he been victorious, would have treated his enemies in the same way. Some editions, indeed, assert that Charles was 'rightly' executed, and though Voltaire affirmed this to be a printer's error and prudently added the remark that the King deserved a better fate, some measure of doubt about his real sentiments may well remain.

The chapter 'On Government' characterises Voltaire's bourgeois liberalism even more clearly. It ignores the whole question of the mechanics of the eighteenth-century English political system. Such details do not worry Voltaire, and in any case a discussion of them might have involved him in arguments about corruption and the bitterness of party strife, which he was anxious to avoid. Instead, he gives us a brief summary of English constitutional history from the time of the Norman Conquest. One of the most interesting features of this account, especially in the light of the current constitutional controversy in France, is that it is equally hostile to absolute monarchs and to feudal magnates. 'Liberty, in England, sprang from the quarrels of tyrants,' says Voltaire, but for this happy result we owe no thanks either to kings or barons, for the motives of both were entirely selfish. If Magna Carta proves anything, it proves that freedom was still almost non-existent. Only with the rise of the Commons and the restriction of both royal and aristocratic power have 'the people' attained liberty. And by 'the people' Voltaire means, as he says, 'the most numerous, the most useful, even the most virtuous and consequently the most venerable part of mankind, consisting of those who study the laws and the sciences; of traders, of artificers'. From this eminently bourgeois description of 'the people', the peasantry are notably absent, though in a revision of 1748, when Voltaire was

71

once again in a militant mood, they were added to the list.

The attack on the feudal privileges still enjoyed by the French aristocracy (and it is these which form Voltaire's real target) is made more explicit in the final paragraphs. The English aristocracy has no power outside the House of Lords, no territorial jurisdiction, no right to administer seigneurial justice, or to hunt at will over the lands of its tenants; the nobility and clergy are not exempt from taxation, which is controlled by the Commons and proportional to income; the peasantry are well clothed and well fed. Finally, the letter on commerce presents the other side of the picture. The aristocracy do not need the protection of feudal privileges because they can, without loss of status, make their fortunes in commerce. Commerce has thus enriched the whole nation and contributed to the growth of liberty. This liberty, in its turn, has caused trade to flourish still more abundantly.

Voltaire's 'bomb' exploded during a period of peace and relative tranquillity, and therefore caused less immediate destruction than might otherwise have been the case. But was it the first to be thrown at the Old Regime? Because of its specifically bourgeois viewpoint, one is inclined to answer this question in the affirmative. Yet in some ways it is less outspoken than an equally successful work which had appeared over a decade earlier.

The *Lettres persanes* had appeared anonymously in 1721, but their authorship did not remain a secret for long. Charles Louis de Secondat, Baron de La Brède et de Montesquieu and President of the *Parlement* of Bordeaux, was then in his early thirties and had already made a modest name for himself, particularly through his contributions – mainly of a scientific nature – to the work of the Academy of Bordeaux. The *Lettres persanes* brought him fame and even (ironically enough, since he had there satirised that august body) membership of the French Academy. It also brought him both a reputation to live up to and one to live down. He never quite succeeded in the second aim, for his reputation as a wit was such that Mme du Deffand, nearly thirty years later, could describe his masterpiece as 'de l'esprit sur les lois'. Wit is not absent from *De l'Esprit des lois*, but it is certainly not its outstanding characteristic. It is, however, the very essence of the *Lettres persanes*.

With remarkable shrewdness, Montesquieu concocted a recipe for success from a number of the best-selling literary techniques of his day. The *Lettres Persanes* was an epistolary novel; it was the finest (though not the first) example of the traveller's tale in reverse — the Persians came to France rather than vice versa. But as it also described an intrigue in the oriental harem which one of the travellers had left behind him, and exploited, at one and the same time, the current predilection for both the exotic and the erotic, it had an even wider appeal. Moreover, though the diversity of the various elements it contains may lead an admirer of classical simplicity to withhold the title of 'masterpiece' from the work, Montesquieu made a powerful attempt to draw them together. The tragic irony of the novel lies in the inability of Usbek, the thoughtful observer of 'Western' life, to show similar wisdom in the treatment of the wives he has left behind him.

The *Lettres persanes* had their more serious side too. Beginning with the celebrated allegory of the Troglodytes (which contains a discussion of the origins and nature of civil society and which may, in considerable part, be interpreted as a refutation of Hobbes), Montesquieu introduced a series of reflections on moral and political problems. Many of the themes he treated were later to be developed in *De l'Esprit des lois*. However, the outstanding feature of the work consists neither in these nor in the harem story, but in the satirical description of France (and, to a lesser extent, of the rest of Europe) during the last years of the reign of Louis XIV and during the Regency. Many of the objects of Montesquieu's satire are trivial foibles of everyday life; Rica, Usbek's fellow-traveller, can portray the grotesque eccentrics of Parisian society in a way which puts one in mind of La Bruyère. Others, however, are of a more serious nature. By putting his words into the mouths of two 'naïve' Persians, Montesquieu enables

73

himself to mock contemporary religious beliefs and political institutions with an openness he would not otherwise have risked. Rica sets the tone early on: Louis XIV is a 'great magician', since he can make his subjects believe that pieces of paper are money; the Pope is an even greater one, since he convinces people that three are one, that bread and wine are not bread and wine, etc. When he comes to deal with the religious disputes and the economic upsets of the Regency, Montesquieu allows his satirical pen even greater freedom; indeed, when he discusses the Inquisition or the disastrous consequences of Law's 'system', satire gives place to rhetorical denunciation. Meanwhile, however, the two Persians have also performed another function. It would have been dangerous for Montesquieu to permit them to denounce openly the Government of Louis XIV and still more the beliefs of the Roman Catholic Church. But they are allowed to fulminate against Turkish despotism which, curiously enough, appears to have marked affinities with the rule of Louis and which, as we are casually informed, the French monarch greatly admired. They are also at liberty to discuss and ridicule some of the more absurd superstitions of the Islamic religion and even to question its more fundamental dogmas. It is, Montesquieu would doubtless assure his critics, purely accidental that the superstitions and dogmas described all have fairly obvious parallels in Christianity.

Because it was a direct (or at any rate a transparent) attack on French religious and political institutions, the destructive effect of the *Lettres persanes* was probably greater than that of Voltaire's *Lettres philosophiques*. Some of its insights into political philosophy (the 'Troglodyte' letters, for example) may also be considered more profound. Yet in terms of practical politics it had no programme to offer. As an aristocrat and a *Parlementaire*, Montesquieu deplored much of what had happened under Louis XIV and the Regent: the former had established royal despotism and the latter had replaced it by social and economic chaos. But when he expressed a nostalgic longing for the conciliar government of the early years of the Regency (a government which had decayed largely through its own inherent weaknesses), he was not offering any very positive alternative to the 'virtuous Troglodytes' of his own day. It is true that many of the seeds of a more positive political attitude are already to be found in the *Lettres*: but as yet they had not come to fruition.

They were not to do so, finally, until the publication of *De l'Esprit des lois* over a quarter of a century later. In the meantime, Montesquieu had discarded his satirical rapier and become a serious student of social and political questions – travelling extensively and then retiring to the relative solitude of his provincial home. In 1734, however, he gave a clear indication of at least one of the ways in which his mind was developing when he published the *Considérations sur les causes de la grandeur des Romains et de leur décadence*. This was one of the first examples of what was later to be called 'philosophical' history: a historical narrative from which the accidental, the anecdotal and the colourful were excluded, which ignored (largely because it rightly assumed they were well known) the annalistic presentation of 'the facts', but which concentrated instead on the general development of social, political and (to a lesser extent) economic institutions, Montesquieu set out to show how the structure of Roman society in the early years was ideally suited to the policy of conquest which the Romans had in fact adopted, but that this same structure was no longer appropriate to the world-wide Empire which Rome later became: hence civil strife, decline and fall. Though others, like, for example, the abbé Dubos, had already prepared some of the ground for it, the *Considérations* was a pioneering work of modern historiography. To this generalisation, however, two important qualifications need to be made: Montesquieu was often rather naïve in the way that he accepted without question all that his 'authorities' told him, and he was sometimes tempted to assert the existence of deterministic principles even when these could not be demonstrated. These same criticisms may, at times, be levelled against *De l'Esprit des lois* itself.

Montesquieu's greatest work finally appeared in

1748. Its impact was summed up at the time by one of the shrewdest of contemporary critics, Baron Grimm, when he remarked that it had 'caused a complete revolution in the spirit of the nation'. The claim is perhaps exaggerated, for the royal Government was not won over (even a 'progressive' like Turgot was profoundly sceptical), opponents like Linguet continued to attack, and sceptics like Voltaire, whilst expressing their admiration, kept on sniping at many of Montesquieu's more exposed positions. In some ways, though, it is an understatement, for Montesquieu's influence rapidly extended beyond the frontiers of his native land: the Scottish Enlightenment would not have been the same without him, nor would the Constitution of the United States of America. The ubiquity of Montesquieu's influence can be measured by the fact that he could include among his fervent admirers men as different as Edmund Burke and Jean-Paul Marat. Clearly *De l'Esprit des lois* was a work of outstanding importance.

Yet the fact that it was admired widely, and by men of such diverse political persuasions, might suggest that its doctrine was not as clear as its author would have wished. As in the case of the *Lettres persanes*, Montesquieu claimed that there was an invisible bond which bound the various parts together, and in the case of both works, the efforts of subsequent critics to reveal the nature of the bond have sometimes been more ingenious than convincing. Yet to say this is not a criticism of *De l'Esprit des lois* itself. Montesquieu was attempting to lay down the guiding principles for the scientific study of society; he was also, in some measure, trying to describe what society *ought* to be like and, in particular, to outline some of the ways in which he thought a society like his own ought to evolve. His work was written over a period of many years and, *méridional* that he was, he often gave himself over to the enthusiasms of the moment. It is hardly surprising that the different parts of his work do not dovetail neatly together and that at times he may be accused of self-contradiction. Yet there are perhaps few works of genius about which similar things could not be said.

76

In his Preface, and in the first book of the work itself, Montesquieu tries to elucidate his aims, methods and principles. His most original contribution, here, is his concept of law. 'Laws,' he asserts at the very beginning, 'are the necessary relationships which derive from the nature of things.' It is primarily (though not exclusively) in this scientific sense that he uses the term, and his object, when studying different forms of society, is to show how these relationships arise and are conditioned: to show the 'spirit' behind the laws.

In many ways this implies a complete break with traditional political and legal theory. Philosophical jurists of earlier centuries had evolved the concept of 'natural law' – certain fundamental principles which, in the light of reason and morality, seemed self-evident. Through the theory of the social contract they had sought to anchor all existing civil societies in this bedrock of natural law. Yet (though there are, of course, many partial exceptions to this generalisation) they had regarded the positive laws of these societies as the more or less arbitrary products of chance, custom, the wisdom of enlightened lawgivers, or the whims of capricious tyrants. Montesquieu wishes to replace such an approach with one which one is tempted to describe as 'Newtonian': with a theory of society based on observation and on an explanatory hypothesis which, when it is supported by sufficient weight of evidence, itself becomes a scientific 'law'.

However, what I have just said must immediately be qualified. For though Montesquieu ignores the theory of social contract, and though the concept of natural law is almost absent from those chapters in which he discusses the various forces which determine social structure and legislation, yet he is unwilling to discard the anchor which had done such valuable service. To do so would be to risk shipwreck on the reefs of naked power and self-interest which Hobbes had charted. So Montesquieu returns, initially at any rate, to the safety of natural law. Concepts of justice and injustice, he asserts, precede positive laws, and to deny this would be as absurd as to claim that, before a circle had ever been drawn, all radii were not equal. Among the

77

'natural laws' to which he immediately draws attention are obedience to the positive laws of one's country, gratitude to one's benefactors, and submission to the will of God. Others, often even more in line with traditional orthodoxy, are mentioned elsewhere in *De l'Esprit des lois*. Moreover, as well as insisting on these natural laws, Montesquieu also insists on the existence of fundamental human instincts. Of these, a desire for peace and a love of sociability are two of the most important (here again he is seeking to exorcise the spirit of Hobbes). The most basic, however, though it only develops with the dawn of reason, is the instinct of religion.

Of course, Montesquieu is taking care not to offend the orthodox, but other texts show that he is not merely paying lip-service to concepts in which he does not believe. These initial principles suggest that his attitude is that of a Cartesian rationalist rather than that of a scientific empiricist. In what he has to say about his method of investigation, moreover, he seems to show similar hesitation between the two approaches: 'I first of all examined all mankind...' he begins, but he continues in a way which suggests that he had already decided exactly what he was looking for: 'I laid down the principles and I saw individual cases conform to them as if of their own accord.' It is not surprising that critics have long argued as to which was his fundamental method. Nor is it surprising that they have come to no agreement, for, as the rest of *De l'Esprit des lois* shows, Montesquieu can, at different times, be both rationalist and empiricist.

It is an oversimplification, though a very convenient one, to say that Montesquieu the Cartesian is most in evidence in the first thirteen books of *De l'Esprit des lois*, and Montesquieu the empiricist in books XIV to XXV. Most of the final books (XXVII, XXVIII, XXX and XXXI) are largely devoted to comments on the Boulainvilliers–Dubois controversy over the question of the Germanic or Roman origin of French society, and to an examination of the origin of feudalism. These, given the importance of the debate to contemporaries, are of considerable significance, yet they are the least

78

relevant of all to Montesquieu's main themes.

In the first thirteen books, Montesquieu discusses the main types of government, the principles on which they are based, and the sort of legislation which is appropriate to, and characteristic of, each type. For him there are three main types of government: the republican (which may be aristocratic, though more usually he thinks of it as democratic), the monarchical, and the despotic. This distinction is not, in itself, particularly original – indeed, with minor modifications, it goes back to Plato. More original, and more important, is Montesquieu's insistence that to each of these forms of government there corresponds a moral and (as we would say) psychological principle which constitutes the dynamic force behind its actions and behind the actions of its citizens. In the case of the republic, this principle is virtue (a word which in Montesquieu's time contained in its meaning a stronger element of 'manliness' than is generally the case today); in the case of a monarchy, it is *gloire* ('glory', here, is an even more inadequate translation, for *gloire* covers a whole range of emotions: pride, dignity, self-esteem, desire for outward recognition, etc.); in the case of despotism (here there are no semantic difficulties) it is fear.

The modern reader may feel that this is just a little too neat and that Montesquieu's categories show a tendency to impose an *a priori* pattern on social phenomena. Similar doubts may also arise in relation to the chapters which follow, for Montesquieu is capable of making rather hasty generalisations on insufficient evidence and is sometimes tempted to replace a description of what, say, 'despotism' is by a more theoretical reconstruction of what the 'ideal' despotism 'ought' to be. Nevertheless, these books, in which he examines the attitudes of his three types of government to a series of problems such as those of education, sumptuary legislation, war and political liberty, constitute a remarkable achievement. They are rich in examples drawn from a wide range of historical and geographical fields, but they illustrate still more clearly Montesquieu's ability to organise the material he has taken over twenty years to amass. They constitute the first

79

real attempt at sociological classification; in them, the apparent chaos of legislation in different societies is, for the first time, reduced to a pattern which is comprehensible on the basis of a small number of initial assumptions.

Yet if Montesquieu's primary aim is to understand the 'spirit of the laws', his investigation is far from being an uncommitted one. The causes of social progress and political liberty, of tolerance and humanity, are ever dear to him. At times, he manifests his sympathies openly, but even when this is not the case, the reader can often sense them. *De l'Esprit des lois* is a work of liberal propaganda as well as social science.

'One cannot speak of these monstrous governments without a shudder,' says Montesquieu in his first chapter on despotism. He later tries to do so, at any rate to the extent of explaining why, in order to survive, despotic governments must be cruel and capricious and must rule through terror. Yet this apparent moderation only makes his condemnation more effective, and hatred of despotism (of which Turkey is his main, though by no means his only, example) is one of the central themes of the whole of *De l'Esprit des lois*.

Democracy and monarchy, on the other hand, both have attractions for him. Like the majority of his contemporaries, he had been nurtured on the heroic legends of the Greek and Roman republics. The ideals of unselfish dedication to the interests of the community, which derive from these examples, are ones of which he approves. This he had shown long ago in the Troglodyte allegory of the *Lettres persanes*, where the wise old man, whom the people had chosen as their first king, laments the fact that they are subjecting themselves to an authority other than that of virtue. He continues to show it in *De l'Esprit des lois*, so much so indeed, that he could appear as a good republican not only to many eighteenth-century disciples but also to some twentieth-century critics. Yet the democratic republic he admires, though it may be an ideal, is a distinctly forbidding one. If the citizens govern the state, it, in its turn, carefully controls their education, regulates most aspects of their behaviour and demands

80

rigorous adherence to its standards of 'virtue'. Montesquieu's democracy is a totalitarian democracy. Moreover, it is not even, in the sense in which the term is most frequently used today, 'democratic': the democracies of which he most approves are those ancient republics which divided their citizens into 'classes' and gave greater political power to those of greater wealth and standing: his ideal is far from being an egalitarian one.

Lastly it is not, at any rate as far as the modern world goes, a practical one. The idea of direct democracy derives primarily from the example of the Greek city states, and can only function effectively in societies which, like them, are small enough to permit direct contact between the great majority of the citizens. In most contemporary European states, as Montesquieu later concedes, republican democracy is impossible.

One may doubt, however, whether he was particularly dismayed by this conclusion. For though he certainly admired the republican ideal, he did so, as it were, from a safe distance. By nature, he was not the sort of man either to preach or to practise the code of austere virtue. Compromise, moderation and tolerance were nearer to his heart, and if he felt the need for reform, he was also, as an aristocrat and a *parlementaire*, deeply attached to the political traditions of his native land. For all these reasons it was with monarchy rather than democracy that his real sympathies lay.

To those nurtured on more recent political slogans, monarchy and despotism might sound suspiciously like the same thing. But in Montesquieu's eyes they were, in principle at any rate, poles apart. Despotism was the arbitrary rule of a single individual who wielded absolute power over the lives and property of his subjects. Monarchy was also the rule of an individual, but of one who governed through intermediate powers and according to fundamental laws. The basic psychological and moral 'principle' behind despotism was fear; monarchy, on the other hand, was permeated by the spirit of *gloire*.

For Montesquieu these were vital distinctions. Yet he was not unaware of the difficulty of maintaining

81

them in practice, faced with a monarch who wished to become a despot. Louis XIV had gone a long way down that slippery slope. Understandably, Montesquieu was preoccupied with erecting barriers to stop his successors sliding in the same direction. If this could be done, then an ideal balance could be achieved, and the unity and singleness of purpose required of the government of a large state could be combined with the continuity of tradition and with respect for liberty (even, within limits, the liberty of political action) of the individual. In consequence, his discussion of monarchy is not merely a description of such monarchies as exist or have existed. It is also propaganda for the type of monarchy which he believes ought to exist. He entitles one chapter: 'Of the excellence of monarchical government.' Yet this excellence was potential rather than actual, and the subsequent history of his own country was to furnish an outstanding example of the failure to realise this potential.

Not that the French monarchy is his only model. In one of the best known, most influential and longest chapters of his work (book XI, ch. vi) he discusses the English constitution. Concerned as he was with the need for intermediate bodies and fundamental laws to limit the powers of monarchy, it is hardly surprising that the government of eighteenth-century England had a strong appeal for him. It was not quite so strong as a reading of this famous chapter might suggest, for in writing it, though he does not explicitly say so, Montesquieu was attempting to reveal the ideal potentialities of the English constitution rather than to describe the English political scene as a whole. During his visit to England, he had found much to criticise in the latter, and he voices some of his criticisms in a later chapter of *De l'Esprit des lois* (book XIX, ch. xxvii). However, the earlier chapter was the one which attracted most attention and which contains the more important aspects of Montesquieu's own political ideas.

It has not proved easy to interpret these. The essence of Montesquieu's thought has traditionally been seen to be the doctrine of the separation of powers – legislative, executive and judicial: liberty could be best assured by a constitutional structure in which no one of these could dominate the others. Yet he himself never uses the phrase 'separation of powers', and though he undoubtedly stresses his belief that they should have some degree of independence, he also points, with apparent approval, to examples of English practice in which this is not the case: the King has a legislative as well as an executive role, and the Parliament can act as a judicial body. What he is most probably advocating is not so much a constitutional separation of powers (though this is in some measure desirable) as the general dissemination of political power throughout the different classes of society. As he points out, there are separate legislative, judicial and executive bodies in the Venetian Republic, but as they are all drawn from the same body of magistrates, this does not prevent the Government of Venice from being tyrannical. In England, on the other hand, all social strata (except the very lowest, and Montesquieu does not dream of enfranchising them) have a part to play. This is why the representative system of the House of Commons is so important, for it gives all citizens of a certain standing some share in the legislative process. This is why juries are so important (he lays more emphasis on them than he does on judges), for through the jury system a significant body of citizens are enabled to play their part in the affairs of the community.

If this chapter is open to more than one interpretation, the same is true of his political ideals as a whole. A conservative monarchist, he believed in the role of the aristocracy, stressed the social necessity of religious institutions (he even defended the Spanish Church!) and spoke of the 'gothic' government (the word was one of Voltaire's favorite terms of abuse) as the best that had ever existed. Yet he hated despotism, cruelty and intolerance, denounced religious persecution (particularly that of the Inquisition) and condemned slavery (though not – at any rate in clear terms – the slave trade which contributed so much to Bordeaux's prosperity). Though he himself was no democrat, his

83

views on representative government prepared the way for much modern democratic thought. And though he was certainly no 'socialist', the views he expressed in his chapter 'Des hôpitaux' (book XXIII, ch. xxix) on the State's responsibility for ensuring the material well-being of its citizens, though they may be seen as the expression of a feudal ideal of community, also look forward to the ideas of Babeuf and Fourier, and to the modern 'welfare state'.

Up to this point I have dealt mainly, though not exclusively, with ideas expressed in the first part of *De l'Esprit des lois*. But with book XIV ('Of laws in the relationship they have with the nature of the climate') Montesquieu's work takes on a completely new tone. Up to this point, he has been trying to show how legislation is determined by the 'nature' and the 'principle' of the Government. However, he seems to have implied, though without explicitly stating it, that these result from an act of will on the part of one or many individuals and that they can therefore, in theory at any rate, be changed by similar acts of will. In the chapter on climate, and in the ones that follow, the role of the psychological and moral 'principle' seems to have vanished. The nature of the individual man, and hence the nature of the society which he evolves, are the necessary physical products of the climate in which he lives. Despotism, for example, is the natural product of hot climates; to condemn it, therefore, is as absurd as smashing the thermometer in order to keep cool. The moral is completely dominated by the material.

Such, at least, is the impression which this and the following chapters would give if they were read on their own. It could be argued that this is how they ought to be read, for they were probably written on their own at a time, relatively early in the genesis of *De l'Esprit des lois*, when Montesquieu was powerfully influenced by theories of climatic determinism, and more particularly by recent medical discoveries of the extent to which climatic conditions determined the spread of infectious disease. And it is certainly true that Montesquieu is forced, by his new attitude, to reverse, or at least to modify, some of his earlier conclusions. Slavery, for example, may be contrary to moral principles, but where does this get us if it can be shown to be the 'natural' product of certain climatic conditions? 'Natural law' itself ceases to be 'natural'.

Yet it would, after all, be a mistake to read these chapters on their own. Though they approach the problem of explaining the nature of laws and social institutions in a way totally different from, and probably more fruitful than, that of the earlier books, they on the whole complement, rather than contradict, what Montesquieu has already said. For the influence of climate, rigorously deterministic as it at first appears, becomes less so when taken in conjunction with what follows. Subsequent chapters examine other determining influences too: those of the nature of the soil, of commerce, of the size of states, of religion. There is a gradual, uneven, but nevertheless significant progression from the determinism of physical causes to that of moral ones. And meanwhile, in book XIX, Montesquieu has made it clear that, important as these determining factors are, their influence is an indirect one. 'Many things,' he remarks in ch. iv, 'govern men: climate, religion, laws, the maxims of the government, the examples of past things, customs, manners; from these is formed a general spirit which is their result.' It is this 'general spirit' which determines the nature of a country's laws, and though this 'general spirit' is itself determined, the process of determination is a complex one, and human will plays its part just as much as do material factors. Hot climates may inevitably make men lazy, but wise legislation can do much to counteract this laziness. The chapters on climatic determinism seem to suggest that material factors have the last word, but Montesquieu was later to assert precisely the opposite, and was to affirm that his argument as a whole demonstrated the perpetual triumph of the moral. If this is so, then despite their radically different approaches, the two main parts of *De l'Esprit des lois* may be considered to form a unity.

This conclusion would have pleased Montesquieu, but to us, perhaps, it does not greatly matter. For the richness of his masterpiece lies primarily in its diver-

sity: in its reflections on a host of historical and sociological problems which there is no space even to mention here; in its ability to provide inspiration for men
as different as Rousseau, Jefferson, Burke and Marat;
in the power of its pleas for traditional attitudes we no
longer find it easy to accept; above all, in its attempt to
develop, for the first time, a scientific method for the
analysis of human society and its institutions.

In the later eighteenth century, political science was
to progress beyond the point where Montesquieu had
left it; but it was to do so very largely along lines which
he had laid down. Political thought in a wider sense,
however, was to be transformed; for men like Rousseau
were to lay the foundations of a modern 'democratic
philosophy' by raising fundamental questions about
the rights of all men, which Montesquieu, conservative
that he was, preferred to keep safely locked away in
Pandora's box. That these questions could be, and indeed had to be, raised was, however, not merely the
result of the growing political and economic tensions
which (partly as a result of disastrous wars) characterised the last decades of the Old Regime in France. It
was also the result of a new philosophy, one which
transformed man's view of his own nature and of the
purpose of his life.

5 A Philosophy for Progress

It was during the eighteenth century that a philosophy *of* progress first took shape. The seeds sown by Fontenelle in the 1680s were finally brought to full fruition in the work of Condorcet over a century later. Yet the naïvely confident optimism which characterises the latter, and which is often attributed to the French Enlightenment as a whole, is in fact shared only by a minority. Diderot, perhaps the most active and extrovert of the *philosophes*, could nevertheless confide to Sophie Volland his conviction that it would have been better never to have been born; Voltaire, though in his more complacent moments he could affirm that he lived in an earthly paradise, saw human history as one long chronicle of stupidity and barbarity; for Rousseau, civilisation was almost synonymous with corruption; and the list could be lengthened almost indefinitely.

Yet if the philosophy *of* progress was the prerogative of a minority, a philosophy *for* progress was probably the most important thing which emerged from the collective thought of the *philosophes*. With varying degrees of conscious commitment, they sought to construct a new universal harmony to replace the fragmented world which had resulted from man's first disobedience. At its centre (and this was probably even true of those who called themselves deists) was man himself. The new philosophy showed him to be a being inherently capable of, and perhaps even predestined to, moral and intellectual improvement. He was the creation of his environment, and as that environment itself improved (and not without some reason, eighteenth-century thinkers believed it *was* improving), so too would he. Alternatively (or sometimes con-

87

currently) his nature derived from a small number of basic instincts. These could be altruistic, like Montesquieu's natural sociability', Voltaire's 'commiseration' or Rousseau's 'pity'. They could be selfish, like sexual desire or the instinct of self-preservation; but Mandeville and others had shown, even at the beginning of the century, that private 'vices' of this nature could be public 'virtues', and more sophisticated utilitarians were soon to appear on the scene, capable of demonstrating that social conformity paid higher dividends than unbridled self-indulgence. What instinct could not be, almost by definition, was 'evil'. It is true that the more perspicacious thinkers had their reservations here; Diderot, for example, though he preached virtue with as much enthusiasm as any religious revivalist, recognised that a man could be 'malheureusement né', and proceeded to deal effectively, if callously, with the problem of any would-be marquis de Sade, by suggesting that the 'malheureusement nés' should either be locked away or liquidated. Generally speaking, however, the *philosophes* were persuaded that 'natural' man was at the worst morally neutral, and more probably positively good.

In so far as they were realists, of course (and the best of them were), they were well aware that historical man was often far from 'good', and they naturally had to attempt to explain why he had fallen from his original state of grace. Critics like Becker have argued that in doing so they were following a line of thought which closely paralleled that of the Christian tradition. This, however, they would themselves have hotly denied, and not without some justification. For the orthodox Christian, the human race (with the exception of the two individuals who originated it) was born 'fallen', and every new-born child, throughout the course of history, inherited his share of original sin. This was a very different thing from asserting that historical conditions had led to the growth of undesirable characteristics in man and society and that these were reproduced, in every subsequent generation, by the influence of environment. The viewpoint of the *philosophes* seemed infinitely more 'scientific'; indeed, it was so, even though the initial premises on which it rested might well seem, to the modern anthropologist, scarcely more acceptable than those of the theologians. However, to examine this debate in the terms in which it was actually conducted is perhaps to miss its point. The *philosophes'* real objection to original sin, and indeed to most forms of Christian orthodoxy, was that they inhibited progress by insisting that, in purely human terms at any rate, it was impossible. Human nature was corrupt, and so too for that matter (if one went back to an older Christian tradition, and confined oneself to the 'sublunary' sphere) was 'inanimate' nature. Such an assumption, which seemed to deny the possibility of any successful human initiative, appeared to the Enlightenment to condemn mankind to stagnation.

Whether the *philosophes* were right is another question. The position of the Church was by no means so completely negative as they often assumed, though even its most outspoken defenders would probably be prepared to admit that its efforts to reconcile human initiative with divine omnipotence involved arguments which were, to say the least, subtle. It could also be argued (and indeed it recently has been) that to start from the assumption that man was originally a savage predator would not only be more accurate than to affirm his natural goodness, but might also lead to a more realistic, and hence more fruitful, appraisal of his real potentialities. This, however, was not the way the eighteenth century saw things. To deny man's natural goodness seemed to the *philosophes* the best way of ensuring that he would never become better.

If man was good by nature, then it seemed to follow that nature, in itself, was also good. Or rather, it might be truer to say that the same psychological and polemical motives which led the *philosophes* to affirm the goodness of man also led them to affirm the beneficence of nature. Those who were deists had, of course, an added reason for doing so, for God was by definition good, and it was logical to suppose that his creation would reflect his personality. It is true that not everyone accepted this position whole-heartedly.

we shall look rather at its philosophical background and, perhaps more important, its sociological and ideological significance.

The cult of nature was, of course, rooted in the achievements of the natural sciences. The universe which the telescope had discovered, and which Newton had reduced from chaos to order, presented a spectacle none could fail to admire; so too, at the other extreme, did the world of the microscopically small. Yet the new glimpses into the infinite which were thus opened might well have led eighteenth-century man, as earlier discoveries had led Pascal, to a heightened sense of his own insignificance and insecurity. Sometimes, indeed, they did, but this was not the general reaction. Two theories, which in their original form seem to contradict each other, but which were to combine to compose an emotional synthesis, turned this spectacle of nature into something reassuring rather than frightening. They were both, in origin, theological. Yet by consistently substituting 'Nature' for 'God', they could, superficially at least, be made to square with more materialistic assumptions.

The first of these was the teleological theory of nature; the belief, not only that man was the 'measure of all things', but that everything in the universe had been consciously created for his benefit. One might perhaps have expected that this theory would be one of the first casualties of the development of scientific method, and certainly Descartes and his disciples had maintained an attitude of absolute hostility to any form of teleological argument. Yet it was to prove remarkably resilient, and in the eighteenth century it in fact gained a new lease of life. In 1711–12, William Derham (Canon of Windsor and Fellow of the Royal Society) delivered the Boyle lectures which were later published under the title of *Physico-Theology: or a Demonstration of the Being and Attributes of God from his Works of Creation*. The work had a European success and was followed by numerous imitations of which the best known (for their intriguing titles, at least) were the *Lithotheologia* and *Insectotheologia* of the German, Lesser. Starting with the atmosphere and

92

ending with plant life, Derham worked his way through nature, demonstrating that it was designed to serve man's interests. However unsatisfactory (or comic) these demonstrations appear to us, they were to be re-echoed, as late as 1784, in Bernardin de Saint-Pierre's *Études de la nature*, and were even to play their part in the nineteenth-century religious revival when Chateaubriand incorporated them into his *Génie du Christianisme*. On the way, they produced further curious offshoots (*Earthquakes Explained and Practically Improved* ran the title of one work published in Edinburgh shortly after the Lisbon disaster of 1755). However, they also influenced the thought of many Christian philosophers and scientists. Among these was Voltaire's Swiss friend, Pastor Élie Bertrand. In his *Mémoires sur la structure intérieure de la terre* of 1752, Bertrand tackled what, for an orthodox Christian who believed the earth roughly six thousand years old, was the somewhat thorny problem of explaining the nature of fossils. They could not, he decided, be the remains of animal or vegetable life, but must have been specially created by God, just as precious stones had been. Why God had done this was more than Bertrand could fathom, but he was teleologically minded enough to conclude that just because we did not know the purpose of fossils, we should not therefore assume that they did not have one. His reasoning, interesting though it is, is unlikely to impress us. However, it did impress Voltaire, who reproduced it almost word for word in one of his many attacks on the idea of the organic origin of fossils. Voltaire, though, made two significant changes. In the first place he substituted 'nature' for 'God'; in the second, he omitted all teleological speculations. The first change revealed that, though he remained (as he always did) an avowed deist, he was quite capable of succumbing to the temptation to personalise the idea of 'nature'. The second showed his unwillingness (characteristic of his common-sense approach) to carry teleological arguments to absurd extremes. Had he not ridiculed these extremes in Pangloss's famous remark that noses were made in order to wear spectacles? Yet this did not mean that he was not prepared to use the arguments themselves. On the contrary, he often did, and he could even talk, in almost Derham-like terms, of the 'utility' of mountains. It was indeed he, more than anyone else, who made teleology a part of 'philosophic' thought. Not that his views went unchallenged. Men like Diderot or d'Holbach, who belonged to the atheist, materialist wing of the 'movement', ridiculed his attachment to 'final causes' almost as much as they did his 'policeman God'. Yet Voltaire's thought, backed both by his unique prestige and his literary gifts, had a powerful influence. To him and his disciples, nature ('under God' as one might say) remained (except, of course, at earthquake-time) 'good'.

This was also the case with many of his opponents. Their attachment, however (and in this they were probably typical of a majority of the *philosophes*), derived from a very different source.

The theory of the 'Great Chain of Being' stemmed ultimately from Plato, but, as Lovejoy has demonstrated in his classic study of the history of the idea, it was to undergo many transformations in the centuries which followed. In the eighteenth, it was almost universally accepted in some form or other, though Voltaire maintained an attitude of down-to-earth scepticism towards it, and in this he had the somewhat surprising support of Samuel Johnson. In essence, in its Christian form at any rate, the theory was an answer to the question why God, who was perfect in himself, had deemed it necessary to create the universe. He had done so, the scholastics argued (and in this Descartes was in agreement with them), because 'existence' was a 'perfection'. It followed that the most perfect universe was the one which gave existence to the maximum number of what Leibniz called 'compossible' beings; and as God could not have done other than wish to create the most perfect possible universe, every such being must exist; every rung of the infinite ladder which stretched from the minutest organism to the most resplendent of the angels must, in fact, be occupied.

94

Man,

> Plac'd in this isthmus of a middle state,
> A being darkly wise and rudely great,

as Pope put it, held a very modest position in this hierarchy. Indeed, the 'Great Chain' theory was often employed by Christian preachers (as it was by Pope himself) to remind man of his relative insignificance, to cure him of the sin of pride, and to persuade him to submit willingly to the limitations which his nature necessarily imposed on him. In this way it could, and indeed did, serve as a corrective to the sentiments most likely to be produced by the teleological theory I have just been discussing.

Belief in the existence of a vast concourse of celestial beings superior to man was, of course, part of the Christian tradition. Eighteenth-century deists, however (not to mention the atheists), were a good deal more sceptical about the omnipresence of angels, even when they were too polite to say so. If the 'Great Chain' theory succeeded in taking this difficulty in its stride, this was largely thanks to the discoveries of the astronomers: beings superior to man, if they were rarely discernible on this planet, might reasonably be supposed to inhabit others among Fontenelle's 'plurality of possible worlds'. Such a transposition already involved a significant degree of secularisation of the theory. A more important development, however, was the one which Lovejoy has called the 'temporalising' of the Chain of Being. If all possible beings coexisted at the same time (as was assumed, if not explicitly stated, in the earlier theory), then change and development were impossible. If, however, the theory was restated in such a way as to suggest that, at some point of time, each potential form of life became actual, then they appeared not merely possible, but, since all potential forms of life manifestly did not exist at the present moment on earth, probable. So the temporalising of the Chain of Being provided a basis for the theory of the evolution of species, and it is no accident that many of those who contributed most to the development of this theory – Maupertuis, Buffon, Diderot and Robinet, for example – were strongly influenced by the idea of the 'Great Chain'.

In this way, what had until recently been a static and conservative world-view mutated into an evolutionary one. The Great Chain became a chain for beings rather than a chain of being. Life, whether at the behest of God, or (as was increasingly assumed) at that of Nature, had climbed link by link from the primeval slime in which Maillet found it to higher things. And though most of these thinkers did not take the trouble explicitly to deny the possible existence of beings higher than man, it was with man, naturally enough, that their positive investigations came to a halt. If there were higher beings in the scale, then in all probability they were yet to evolve. And so man became once again 'the measure of all things', while Nature herself became a beneficent and active force to which it was increasingly easy to assign many of the qualities previously attributed to God. There were many, moreover, to whom the distinction between the two appeared meaningless, for Spinoza's influence was widespread in eighteenth-century France, and though thoroughgoing pantheists were few, the Spinozist equation of God with nature, which had so shocked his contemporaries, now found echoes everywhere.

Man was good, Nature was good, and a fundamental harmony existed between them. Such was the creed the *philosophes* proclaimed, even though, having proclaimed it, most of them immediately started making reservations. Whether they really believed what they said is another matter. For basically, what they were doing was constructing an anti-creed: a series of intellectual positions from the safety of which they could effectively combat what Voltaire was to call *l'infâme*. By this they meant traditional orthodox Christianity, but more especially certain aspects of it: its belief in a jealous God and in the radically corrupt nature of man; its advocacy of 'Old Testament' morality; its intolerance, its asceticism and its claim to authority over all fields of knowledge. For them, Christianity was above all the enemy of progress, and it was for progress

96

that they cared most. Philosophically speaking, many of the concepts I have just been discussing will not stand up to very close scrutiny. The shrewder minds among the *philosophes* were probably aware of this, but it did not worry them unduly. 'I write in order to act,' said Voltaire; and a great deal of the speculative philosophy of the Enlightenment can also be regarded as essentially a prelude to action.

The same may probably be affirmed about another of their central themes, one which I shall only mention here, though it has recently been the subject of the thesis running into many hundreds of pages: the cult of happiness. The list of works written in eighteenth-century France to prove that happiness was the goal of life is a very long one, and the facile generalisations often made about the nature of happiness and the ease with which it may be attained often seem calculated to irritate rather than console ordinary suffering mortals. They could produce similar reactions at the time too, as can be seen from the example of Diderot's indignant denunciation of Helvétius' attempt, in *De l'Homme*, to explain his subject in the crudest terms, as a pleasure-seeking animal. Yet the *philosophes* were not usually themselves practitioners of crude hedonism, even when they preached it. And of which of them could one unhesitatingly affirm that he was a happy man: La Mettrie? Voltaire? Rousseau? Diderot? They all had their periods of despair, even though they usually continued to proclaim that happiness was the aim of life. Some, it is true, had their momentary doubts. Voltaire, for example, in his little *conte* entitled *Histoire d'un bon Bramin*, contrasted the self-questioning and the sufferings of his Indian philosopher (who was manifestly a self-portrait) with the serene happiness of his neighbour, a stupid *dévote*, and asked the question: Would I change places with her? The fact that he felt compelled to answer the question in the negative puzzled him. Was not happiness the aim of life? 'There is a lot to be said about this,' he concluded; but he never said it.

Perhaps he never said it because he felt, on reflection, that it should not be said. Or perhaps, after all, he did say it, or something very similar, at the time of the Lisbon earthquake. Even then, however, he felt the need to add a note of hope to the otherwise gloomy ending of the poem, and later, as we have seen, he was to revert to a far more optimistic attitude. And perhaps he was 'morally' right to do so. To deny that the pursuit of happiness was the aim of life was, in terms of the practical politics of the eighteenth century, to range oneself on the side of those for whom life not merely was, but ought to be, a vale of tears. To affirm it, on the other hand, however naïvely and unconvincingly, was to espouse the cause of progress. Like the belief in the natural goodness of man and of nature, eighteenth-century hedonism formed part of an ideological framework which, to the contemporary mind, seemed to allow man the best chance of improving his lot.

This inquiry into the French Enlightenment started with a number of basic concepts such as reason, experience and scientific method. In this chapter they have had a very minor role, and the philosophy I have been describing appears every bit as speculative as those which the earlier *philosophes* so roundly condemned. I have tried to show that these speculations are linked, as was the empiricists' assault on tradition, with a concern for progress. Nevertheless, if they constituted the essence of Enlightenment philosophy, its critics would be fully justified in not taking it too seriously. They do not do so, however, as the chapters which follow will show.

6 Sensationalism, Scientific Materialism and Evolution

In turning to those aspects of the thought of the *philosophes* which are much nearer to what we usually think of as 'philosophy', we are not altogether abandoning the subject of the preceding chapter. Sensationalism, too, was a philosophy for progress. Its principal creator spoke of himself as 'employed as an under-labourer ... in removing some of the rubbish that lies in the way to knowledge'. Such modesty was characteristic of him, yet in reality Locke was doing much more than merely preparing the ground; he was trying to construct a science of the human mind on the basis of Newtonian principles. His principal French disciple, Étienne Bonnot de Condillac, pursued this aim even more openly, and indeed could accuse Locke of not being 'Newtonian' enough. Moreover, the sensationalism they created and developed was later to provide the essential psychological and philosophical starting-point for the theory *of* progress; Helvétius, Turgot and Condorcet were all to build their imposing, if fragile, castles on the ground which Locke and Condillac had cleared for them.

The youngest son of an aristocratic family from Dauphiné, Condillac studied in Paris, became (like many younger sons of noble families) an *abbé*, and then (like many well-connected *abbés*) entered the high society of the capital. He had many friends among the more 'advanced' *philosophes*, beginning with his brother, Mably, and including Rousseau, Diderot and d'Alembert. Despite this, however, and despite the fact that he prosecuted his 'Newtonian' study of human nature with considerable fervour, he remained, in many ways, a man apart. Though he has been called 'le philosophe des *philosophes*', he did not share in a

99

number of the characteristic activities of the majority of the *philosophes* themselves: he remained an orthodox, if not particularly fervent, Catholic; in politics, he was a conventional conservative monarchist; he was considered 'respectable' enough to be appointed tutor to Louis XV's nephew, the Prince of Parma, and this at a time (1758) when those who claimed to be his disciples were being increasingly persecuted.

His very independence was perhaps one of the reasons why he became 'le philosophe des *philosophes*': they could quote him as an authority free from the taint of heresy. His reputation as a philosopher, however, was probably a more important reason; for among the *philosophes* (and despite the reservations mentioned above, he *may* be classed among them) he comes nearest to being what we today might call a 'professional' philosopher. After he got to Parma, he spent much of his time composing an encyclopedic (though, on the whole, rather unadventurous) *Cours d'études* for the Prince. Before that, however, his reputation was based almost entirely on his philosophical writings.

The first of these was the *Essai sur l'origine des connaissances humaines* of 1746. Yet it is more appropriate to begin a discussion of his ideas with the *Traité des systèmes* of 1749, for this work contains the fullest statement of his general principles. In it, he takes up Locke's task of 'removing the rubbish' from the philosopher's path. He is, however, no modest 'under-labourer', but rather a confident engineer equipped with dynamite and concrete; the dynamite is for blasting away the metaphysical systems of the seventeenth century; the concrete is for laying down a new scientific basis for the systematic understanding of man and nature.

Condillac's objections to the seventeenth-century metaphysicians often echo criticisms to be found in Locke. In the *Traité*, however, they are more effective because they are more concentrated. Descartes, Malebranche, Spinoza, Leibniz (together with the lesser-known Boursier) are weighed, one by one, in Condillac's methodological balance and are found wanting: Descartes built his theory of knowledge on the errone-

100

ous concept of innate ideas; Malebranche (whom Condillac held in relatively high esteem) explained the workings of the mind by metaphors and then proceeded to take his metaphors literally; Spinoza used the meaningless vocabulary of traditional metaphysics; Leibniz, on the other hand, created a new vocabulary of his own, but this was no better, since its meaning was obscure and its utility doubtful. All these metaphysicians were tarred with the same brush: they invented systems which they then applied to nature, rather than trying to discover the systems of nature itself.

Much of the *Traité des systèmes* is an elaboration of these criticisms. In the concluding chapters, however, Condillac turns to more positive matters. He is enough of a sceptic and an empiricist to doubt whether man will ever be capable of explaining *the* system of nature; but he is enough of a rationalist and a Christian to believe that nature has a logical structure and that, being God's creation, it forms a unity. Between the extremes of doubt and over-confidence, however, there lies the path traced by Newton. The Newtonian system (by which Condillac means, above all, the law of attraction and the consequences derived from it) is (in both senses of the word) a 'true' system. It is based on observed and experimentally verifiable facts, and every part of it conforms to, and follows from, these facts. The Newtonian method may not lead to an explanation of the universe *in toto*; but it provides the key to a systematic understanding of at least some of its parts.

Both the earlier *Essai sur l'origine des connaissances humaines* and Condillac's next important work, the *Traité des sensations* of 1754, are attempts to apply this Newtonian method to the study of the human mind and the problem of knowledge. Whether they in fact succeed may be questioned. The phenomena which Condillac set out to explain do not in reality lend themselves to the same sort of objective and empirical observation as do (or, at any rate, did) those of astronomy. Moreover, Condillac, unlike Newton, knew exactly what he was looking for, and his desire to discover a law as simple and universal as Newton's may well have tempted him to gloss over objections to the one he thought he had found; he was, after all, human. Nevertheless, whatever its deficiencies, Condillac's theory was coherent and convincing enough to survive almost unchallenged for half a century; it was not until the advent of Maine de Biran that a serious criticism of its fundamentals was to emerge.

That 'the *materials* of reason and knowledge' came from experience was, of course, one of the main contentions of Locke's *Essay*. It is, however, significant that Locke italicised the word 'materials'. For though he attacked what he called 'innate ideas' and compared the mind to 'white paper, void of all characters', he did not think (at least not consistently) of mind as a purely passive recipient of experience. It was not full of innate ideas, but it had innate qualities, or faculties, such as will, judgement, memory and imagination. Whence did these derive? Locke did not ask, let alone answer, this question, but Condillac felt it imperative to do both, for a mind full of unexplained 'faculties' seemed to him only a little less unsatisfactory than one stocked with 'innate' ideas. To arrive at 'Newtonian' simplicity, one had to explain these faculties, too, in terms of experience. It was primarily to this task that he addressed himself, and he did so with considerable success. Not with absolute success, perhaps, for even Condillac had to admit that there was some active, and presumably innate, principle lurking in the mind, one to which, following the example of Locke, he gave the name of *inquiétude*. With this exception, however, the understanding itself, as well as its contents, derived from sensation.

In the *Essai sur l'origine des connaissances humaines*, Condillac first formulated his answer to the problem of the origin of man's power of reflection, which Locke had largely ignored. He began with pure consciousness, i.e. awareness of sense-impressions. The first step in the awakening of the mind was the development of what he termed 'attention' – a gradually increasing awareness that certain sensations were associated with pleasure and others with pain. 'Attention' thus led naturally to the development of a mental mechanism

102

which Condillac called (though he by no means invented the phrase) 'the association of ideas'. It was in this principle that he found his equivalent of the Newtonian law of attraction. As experience gradually increases, more ideas are associated and they form longer connected chains. When the mind 'attends to' the first link in such a chain, the others will begin to follow automatically, even when the sense-data which originally provoked them are absent. This, for Condillac, was the beginning of self-awareness (which, unlike Locke, he did not regard as innate) and hence of memory and the other 'faculties of the mind'.

Before these can come into existence, however, they must be provided with material which they can handle, and the 'raw' data of sense-experience do not provide this. Abstraction and classification, not to mention the more advanced forms of reasoning, presuppose the existence of mental symbols, i.e. of language. If the principle of the association of ideas provided Condillac with his first key to the way in which the understanding developed, it was still necessary for him to explain the birth of language, for without such an explanation, the concept of the 'innate' – which he was so eager to exclude from his argument – was merely transferred to what was logically, if not necessarily temporally, a later stage in this process of development. Condillac's discussion of the origin of language, which occupies much of the central section of the *Essai*, constituted one of the first attempts of the eighteenth-century philosophers to solve what was, for any naturalistic interpretation of man's development, a vital problem. Many others, like Rousseau, Maupertuis or Turgot, were later to follow in his footsteps. His only important predecessor, however (to whom, as he acknowledged, he was much indebted), was William Warburton, Bishop of Gloucester, whose voluminous *Divine Legation of Moses* (1738–41), a curious synthesis of the geometric spirit and Christian apologetics, was in its day widely influential.

Condillac's explanation of the growth of language involved recourse to another 'innate' instinct, but one which he regarded as physical rather than mental in

103

origin: man's capacity for self-expression. Language, he argued, originated in the sounds and gestures which naturally accompanied certain feelings of pleasure, pain, surprise, etc. Only later, as a result of the workings of the principle of the association of ideas, did these sounds and gestures begin to be used as a means of communication. Only much later still, though by an extension of the same process, did man begin to create names for the commonest objects and, finally, to formulate generic and abstract terms. Just how long the stages in this process actually took, Condillac does not attempt to indicate, which is perhaps fortunate when one stops to consider that he was, ostensibly at any rate, working within the limits of the time-scale provided by a literal interpretation of the Old Testament.

Condillac's theory was to form the basis of most of the eighteenth-century discussion of the origin of language, and even today it is not without its adherents (witness, for example, R. G. Collingwood). In its context, however, it provided the final step in a psychological explanation of the development of mind which was remarkably coherent. Nevertheless, it had its ambiguities and its lacunae, and of these Condillac was not unaware. So, in the *Traité des sensations*, he tried to set forth what were basically the same arguments, but with greater rigour. In the first place, he attempted to clarify his epistemological position. So far, I have avoided discussing this, and have presented Condillac's views in terminology consistent with a basically materialist world outlook and a 'correspondence' theory of knowledge: one, that is, which assumed that sensations were 'caused by' a 'real' world of objects outside the human mind. This, after all, was how most of his disciples interpreted him. Yet it is by no means clear that this is what he really thought, and there are passages in the *Essai* which flatly contradict such an interpretation and affirm that sensations are purely mental phenomena. In these circumstances, a 'correspondence' theory of knowledge was impossible (since there was nothing to correspond to), and the only tenable theory was a 'coherence' one based on order *within* the mind. Nor could there be any proof of the existence of 'minds' other than one's own, and Condillac's arguments, as Diderot pointed out in his *Lettre sur les aveugles*, seemed to lead towards complete solipsism. To judge from the *Traité*, however, this was not Condillac's intention, for in the later work he moved a considerable way towards a more consistent position of environmental determinism. Yet this did not involve the adoption of a clearly materialist position, and Condillac was still careful to maintain a distinction between physical 'senses' and mental 'sensations'. He was, no doubt, anxious to avoid the accusation of 'naïve' materialism, primarily because he considered such a view to be incorrect, but also, very probably, in order to avoid antagonising ecclesiastical authority. Certainly, in his next major work, the *Traité des animaux*, also published in 1754, he was to criticise the 'transformist' views of Buffon from what was, to the theologians, a reassuringly orthodox standpoint.

The *Essai* had left a number of other problems unsolved: At what stage in his development did man become aware of his own identity? Was it possible to explain mental phenomena such as that of volition in purely sensationalist terms? Above all, was it possible to establish a clear relationship between the different forms of sense data? The last of these questions had constituted one of the most important problems in epistemology ever since Berkeley's *New Theory of Vision*, and Diderot's *Lettre sur les aveugles* of 1749 had recently revived interest in it. The *Traité des sensations* sought to resolve all these difficulties.

It did so through the medium of the hypothesis with which Condillac's name is now most closely associated: that of the statue. Originally inert and mindless, the statue was endowed, one by one, with all the five human senses. Condillac attempted to show, by a method which has been called one of 'imaginative analysis', that sense-impressions lay at the root, not merely of all knowledge, but of all the faculties of the mind. The method was perhaps not quite so 'Newtonian' as he himself imagined, since it was partly based on the sort of introspection for which no experimental verification was possible; yet given its limita-

105

tions (which were those of eighteenth-century science) it was highly effective. To begin with, Condillac gave his statue a single sense – that of smell – and showed that, provided one accepted the existence of Locke's initial positive feeling of 'uneasiness', it was possible to demonstrate how the statue would develop, even though only in rudimentary form, the faculties of mind which Locke had assumed to be innate. Not only would repeated contact with different odours (pleasant and otherwise) teach it to classify them, but it would also stimulate memory (the argument, here, is less convincing) and finally, judgement. However, it was only with the acquisition of the other senses that these faculties were developed, and certain aspects of human knowledge and personality could only arise at a later stage. Though in the *Traité*, Condillac was careful to avoid the solipsistic positions of the *Essai*, in another way he moved closer to Berkeley, for he insisted that self-awareness, together with consciousness of the 'otherness' of the outside world, could not arise from smell, hearing or sight, but only came into existence when the statue acquired touch and movement. It was then that it learnt to attribute material reality to the external sources of its sensations. Yet though Condillac regarded this final step as 'natural', he did not himself consider it a logically justifiable one. Though he provided a basis for a consistently materialist philosophy, his own position remained, like Locke's, a predominantly idealist one.

Because of its 'Newtonian' simplicity as much as for the thoroughness of its analytical argument, Condillac's sensationalism was to be accepted without challenge by the majority of the later *philosophes*. Yet if no one felt capable of refuting it, it probably produced a certain amount of 'uneasiness' even among some of its disciples. For the most characteristic attribute of the statue – and hence of the man it symbolised – was its passivity. In the *Traité*, even more than in the *Essai*, Condillac seemed to have portrayed man as a being who was the inactive creature of his environment. In some ways, it may be argued, this was a 'liberating' view, since it did not merely explain human nature in comprehensible terms but also contained the seeds of the argument, which Helvétius and others were later to develop, that by improving the environment one could improve man. However, there was little hint of such reformism in Condillac himself, and the statue-man he had described seemed too passive a creature to possess the driving force necessary to initiate such a transformation. For a 'philosophy for progress', something more positive was needed to supplement pure sensationalism.

It could have come from a reappraisal of the nature of will, or, as later happened, with Maine de Biran's critique of orthodox sensationalism, from an insistence on the primacy of the mind's awareness of its own body and its control over it. Yet in so far as it did come in the eighteenth century, it came, ironically enough, not from some form of philosophical idealism, but from a current of thought which owed a great deal to one of the most outspoken materialists of the age: La Mettrie. This affirmation is difficult to substantiate, for La Mettrie was a man who loved to shock his readers and was eminently successful in his attempts to do so. He was to be vilified not only by the theologians and doctors whom he attacked but also by nearly all the philosophes themselves, including Voltaire, d'Alembert and the man who ought to have been best fitted to appreciate the value and novelty of his ideas – Diderot. Practically no one, in France at any rate, was prepared to acknowledge his influence. Yet the fact that he was frequently refuted (at a time when his books – banned almost everywhere – were little read) suggests that, like Hobbes and Spinoza in the previous century, his arguments troubled (or perhaps even inspired) a fair number of people who were unwilling to admit it.

Julien Offroy de La Mettrie was born in 1709 and was, like another of the more profound scientific thinkers of the age, Maupertuis, a native of Saint-Malo. After studies in Paris, Rheims and Leyden, he became a doctor in his native town. Later he became an army medical officer, serving during the War of the Austrian Succession and witnessing battles like Dettingen and Fontenoy. In 1745 he published his first major work, the *Histoire naturelle de l'âme*, a book which was obviously materialist in inspiration and which was soon to be burnt on the orders of the *Parlement* of Paris. At the same time, he antagonised another influential body, the medical profession, by his satirical *Politique du médecin de Machiavel* of 1746. He soon found it expedient to seek refuge in Holland, and it was there that he published his most famous work, *L'Homme machine* (1747). This led to further persecution, and La Mettrie fled to Berlin, where Maupertuis headed the Academy, and where he soon became one of the close companions of Frederick the Great. There he published his last works, among which *Le Système d'Épicure* of 1750 was probably the most significant. In 1751, much to the delight of his enemies, who thought such an end appropriate for an outspoken hedonist and materialist, he died after indulging too freely in truffled game *pâté*.

Though he had already written a good deal on medical matters, the *Histoire naturelle de l'âme* was his first venture into the realms of philosophy. In a way, it was also his last, for it had the appearance of a 'serious' philosophical treatise, whereas in later works he was to return to a much freer and more personal style. In it he put forward the idea which was henceforth to remain at the centre of his doctrine: the 'soul' was simply a modification of matter. The primary sources of this conviction were probably to be found in his own medical experience. However, he chose to express himself (whether from conviction, or in the hope of avoiding censure) in the traditional language of Aristotelian scholasticism. The resulting compromise, as he himself was quick to realise, was not a happy one, and when he came to write *L'Homme machine*, he dispensed with the formalism and substituted Descartes for Aristotle. Descartes, of course, whilst demonstrating the mechanical nature of the body, had insisted that the 'soul' was a totally different substance. But La Mettrie brushed aside this distinction, asserting that Descartes had only make it in order to avoid antagonising the theologians. He defended Descartes, too, against those who ('aping Locke', as he said) attacked

108

him for his reliance on 'innate ideas'; these, according to La Mettrie, were peripheral rather than central to the Cartesian view of man.

Yet if La Mettrie claims to be returning to Descartes, he does so, in reality, only to a limited degree. The title of *L'Homme machine* was a late choice, and one which was probably intended to be provocative. However, it may well give a false impression of the book itself, if it is taken to imply that La Mettrie's primary concern is with the levers, pulleys and furnaces which constitute the human organism. It is true that he does make use of these mechanical analogies, but he does so only sparingly, and largely because (since biochemistry was as yet unheard of) he had no other vocabulary at his disposal. The aim of *L'Homme machine* is far from being that of showing that man is a 'mechanism' in this narrow sense of the term.

It aims, in the first place, to show that the relations between 'body' and 'soul' are so close that it is both unnecessary and unreasonable to suppose they have a separate identity. Here, La Mettrie draws as much on his experiences as an army surgeon as on his reading for evidence of the extent to which the mind can be transformed by what happens to the body. His observations are presented with a rapidity and enthusiasm which may carry the reader with him, though his argument is somewhat lacking in rigour, and does not pause to take account of the objections which might be raised by a philosophical idealist. He proceeds, in the next stage of his demonstration, to show that man does not differ essentially from other members of the animal kingdom. His superiority to the higher apes results largely from the gift of speech, and La Mettrie speculates hopefully on the possibility of teaching monkeys to talk. Many animals unquestionably exhibit signs of intelligence akin to that of humans, and the fact that they are also able to feel remorse is an indication that they, no less than man, feel the promptings of conscience and hence of 'natural law'.

Up to this point there is little that is very new in his argument apart from its tone of confident affirmation. He becomes more original when he supports his views

109

with evidence drawn from more recent discoveries in biology and physiology. In the first place, he has been profoundly impressed (like many of his contemporaries) by Trembley's account of the ability of certain types of polyp to regenerate completely new beings from each of the severed portions of an original one. He was equally conscious (and probably the first to be so) of the implications of Haller's study of the so-called principle of muscular irritability: living muscle continued to react to certain stimuli even when separated from any contact with a 'controlling' brain. In fact, though he continued to call man a machine, La Mettrie was introducing into the traditional mechanistic view of human and animal life a new vitalism. The severed muscle or the dismembered polyp illustrated by their activity the existence of a purposive 'force' in living matter. Such a view was remote from that of Descartes, for whom animal mechanism was a 'dead' mechanism. It was also far removed from the position of Condillac, whose statue-man was almost totally passive. This is made even more clear when we consider what La Mettrie has to say about man himself. He stresses that individuals are what they are, not because of their environment but because of their organisation – which depends primarily on heredity. Human nature is characterised by positive qualities such as imagination rather than by a simple ability to receive and correlate sensations.

Compared with Condillac's *Essai* or *Traité*, *L'Homme machine* is a very short work. Moreover, though an informed and sympathetic study like that of Adam Vartanian brings out its full significance, it often fails to make its own points very clearly. This is partly explained by the fact that La Mettrie lacked the mastery of literary style which characterised so many of the leading scientific writers of the age. Yet his informality, reminiscent of that of Diderot, is often more attractive to the modern reader than are the polished periods of, say, a Buffon. So, too, is the open-mindedness he often exhibits: though a convinced materialist, he is quite prepared to admit the strength of the arguments in favour of a creator God, and even the idea of

110

personal immortality seems to him one that he has no right to reject.

Condillac had many disciples; La Mettrie appeared to have none, though Diderot, and later d'Holbach, probably owed him far more than they ever admitted. Yet in a way, it was with La Mettrie rather than Condillac that the future was to lie. For, despite the title of his best-known work, he was one of the main initiators of a movement away from the mechanical sciences towards the biological ones. In his *Système d'Épicure*, he went even farther in this direction than in *L'Homme machine* itself and produced one of the more important early sketches of a theory of organic evolution. And it was with the biologists and evolutionists that the future lay. Newtonianism, it is true, continued to dominate the physical sciences and even to inspire (though not always with happy results) attempts to solve problems in other fields. But the Newtonian universe was a static one, governed by immutable laws, and once these laws had been discovered (as they had been by Newton himself), no further great leap forward in the understanding of the physical world took place. It was in the sciences which dealt with a changing world, such as geology and palaeontology, and still more in the life-sciences such as biology and (though less obviously) sociology, that the most striking advances were made. The Newtonian method sometimes contributed to this process; but it often proved of little help, and may even, at times, have been positively harmful. The rift between the approaches characteristic of these two different forms of scientific inquiry has recently been highlighted in a study by C. Kiernan, but, despite outstanding exceptions such as Diderot, it was not apparent to most eighteenth-century thinkers. Yet the development of evolutionary thought which characterised the life-sciences brought about a profound change in the nature of the Enlightenment. It may even be said to have played a vital part in its final overthrow by (or perhaps one ought rather to say its final transformation into) what we now call 'Romanticism'.

The wind of change blew most strongly among the

biologists, for it was they who could make best use of man's newest tool – the microscope. Most of them, however, also shared a belief in the Great Chain of Being theory, and their search for further links in the chain led them, as we have seen, to transform the theory from a static into an evolutionary one. It is true that there were powerful forces working against such a change. Linnaeus, possibly the greatest of eighteenth-century biologists, was primarily concerned with the classification of species, and his work and reputation tended to reinforce the static approach. So too did the most generally accepted theory of heredity which was one of *emboîtement*, or pre-formation: the seeds of future generations were all contained, like an endless series of Russian dolls, in the wombs of the animals which God had originally created. This theory had the backing of the Church, and was naturally accepted by those biologists (and they were numerous and often distinguished) who held orthodox religious views. Transformist ideas, when they began to appear, also seemed to be refuted by the sterility of the offspring which resulted from the mating of members of two different species. Even Buffon, who was at times pre-pared to embrace the evolutionary hypothesis, found this fact a serious stumbling-block.

Yet though these traditional theories continued to find support, the balance was being tipped against them. Trembley's *Mémoires* on the fresh-water polyp appeared in 1744, and their proof that nature possessed hitherto unsuspected powers of regeneration clearly demanded a fresh look at many established theories; we have seen the use La Mettrie made of them. Even more important, however, was the work of John Need-ham, whose *New Microscopical Discoveries* was pub-lished in 1745 and soon translated into French. What Needham had 'discovered' was nothing less than the spontaneous generation of life from dead vegetable matter, and if his conclusions were correct, then the whole science of biology had obviously to be rebuilt on a new basis. In fact, Needham had taken insufficient precautions to ensure that his samples of dead matter were completely sterile. This, however, was only to be

112

demonstrated (by Spallanzani) some twenty years later, and in the meantime biologists and philosophers were presented with a far more thoroughgoing basis for a totally materialist theory of life than that contained in Locke's tentative suggestion that it was not beyond God's powers to endow matter with thought. Diderot, among others, was, as we shall see, ready to take advantage of the situation.

Needham himself was not, for he remained a very orthodox Catholic. Nor was the greatest of the Frenchmen with whom he had close contact. Georges Louis Leclerc, comte de Buffon, curator of the *Jardin du Roi*, was not the sort of man to seek martyrdom, and was, if not a sincere Catholic, at any rate a convinced deist. Yet he was prepared to go some of the way with the transformists; far enough, certainly, to provoke refutations from Condillac and others and to incur the wrath of the Sorbonne. He also lent his authority to other evolutionist theories, asserting, for example, in his *Théorie de la Terre* of 1749, that the planetary system could well have come into existence as a result of attraction between the sun and some passing star, claiming that the earth itself had evolved over a vast period of time and that man had existed for tens of thousands of years.

Such views shocked the orthodox, as did many others which appeared in the later volumes of Buffon's monumental *Histoire naturelle*, publication of which was only completed after his death in 1788. Yet they were cautious and moderate compared with many that had already appeared. For in their assault on the static universe, the evolutionary biologists had soon been joined by the palaeontologists. The discovery of marine fossils in areas far removed from the sea had at first been hailed as a vindication of the biblical story of Noah's Flood, but, unfortunately for the theologians (whose perplexed reaction is exemplified by the already-mentioned arguments of Pastor Élie Bertrand), fossils were soon found in large quantities in widely separated geological strata. In 1720, in a memoir on the marine fossils found in the *faluns* of Touraine, Réaumur argued that such deposits could only have been laid down over an immense period of time, and concluded that the Atlantic, or a branch of it, must at one time have covered the whole of this area, leaving Brittany as an island. From such an assertion, it needed only a relatively short imaginative step to arrive at the conclusion that the whole earth had at one time possessed a similar watery surface. Bernard de Maillet, a speculative thinker of no mean calibre, took this step, and others too. His most important work was published posthumously in 1748, and as its title is both long and explanatory, it seems worth while to quote it in its English version. *Telliamed* (devotees of crossword puzzles will have little difficulty in interpreting this); *or Discourses between an Indian Philosopher and a French Missionary on the Diminution of the Sea, the Formation of the Earth, the Origin of Men and Animals* made the first significant synthesis of the new information provided by geologists, palaeontologists and biologists. Maillet's world had been originally covered by sea, which had gradually evaporated (and was still doing so) leaving and forming the land continents. Life, as the existence of marine fossils proved, had originally developed in the sea, and as it diminished, land animals had evolved. Maillet is not very clear as to just how this happened, for on the one hand he thinks of fairly rapid and dramatic transformations such as that of a chrysalis into a butterfly, whilst, on the other, he maintains a belief in a certain fixity of species: man, for example, has probably developed from an original merman.

The middle years of the century witnessed a ferment of evolutionary speculation. Among the most important contributors to it, other than those I have already mentioned, was Maupertuis. He had been the greatest of the French Newtonians, but, significantly enough, in the forties, he turned his attention from the mechanical to the biological sciences and produced important studies of inheritance and significant arguments for transformism, as well as a number of rather fanciful speculations which were to be the target of Voltaire's wit. It can indeed be argued that the majority of the pieces of the Darwinian jigsaw were available by the sixties. Yet though there were moments when men like Maupertuis, and more particularly Diderot, appeared to be fitting them together correctly, they were always allowed to fall apart again. The transformists' failure to achieve a 'breakthrough' to a consistent theory of evolution may partly be explained by their continuing tendency to think in what René Hubert has called 'biblical categories'. In particular, when they had arrived at a concept of 'natural selection', they were prone to think of it as a process by which, at the dawn of history, the ill-adapted species had been weeded out, instead of envisaging it as something continuous. Otherwise, they might well have produced a more coherent doctrine and one which might have been generally accepted. As Norman Hampson has pointed out in an illuminating chapter in his study of the Enlightenment, the climate of thought of eighteenth-century France was much more in tune with the doctrine of *The Origin of Species* than was that of Victorian England.

The historical Pyrrhonism exemplified by Pierre Bayle had been one of the principal weapons used by the early Enlightenment in its attack on tradition, and more particularly on the traditions of orthodox Christianity. One might well expect that the revolutions in geology and biology, together with the new concepts of human nature provided by materialists and sensationalists, would have resulted in a corresponding metamorphosis in historiography. Indeed, they probably did, but not, on the whole, until a much later date. It is true that the outline of a theory of historical progress is already found in the *Discours* which the young Turgot delivered at the Sorbonne in 1750, but, as we shall see, no one took much immediate notice of it. Other important advances in what later came to be called 'the philosophy of history' – those associated with Vico and Herder, for example – originated outside France, and had very little immediate influence on French thought. Contrary to a frequently expressed view, however, interest in history was very much alive in eighteenth-century France. Yet the most prominent figures – from Fréret to Foncemange or Sainte-Palaye (who rehabili-

115

tated the despised Middle Ages) – tended to be anti-
quarians, or, like Boulainvilliers and Dubos, politicians in disguise. The influence of Montesquieu, important though it was, produced sociologists rather
than historians, and the greatest of these were Scots or
English, rather than French.

However, there is a more positive side to the picture.
The dimensions of history were enlarged, partly as a
result of an increased knowledge of countries and civilisations outside Europe and still more by the rejection
of biblical chronology and the scientists' discoveries
about the age of the world and the probable immense
antiquity of the human race. It is true that historians
were ill-equipped to know what to do with these tens of
hundreds of thousands of years which had suddenly
been placed at their disposal, for archaeology was in its
infancy, and the study of pre-history had barely been
conceived. In his *Philosophie de l'histoire* of 1765
(which now forms the introduction to the *Essai sur les
mœurs*) Voltaire used these additional centuries
largely as a stick with which to administer a further
beating to the already moribund chronology of the
Bible. Yet even earlier, in his *Discours sur l'inégalité* of
1755, Rousseau had made a more positive use of the
new freedom in order to temporalise the previously
static 'state of nature', and to demonstrate that man
had probably already made a long and complex jour-
ney before arriving at the beginning of civil society.
Rousseau's work, however, as he himself freely recognised, was a series of brilliant intuitions rather than a
study of historical fact. The man who did more than
any other to give positive substance to the 'Enlightenment' view of history never lost sight of the facts. Voltaire may not have been a great systematic or speculative thinker, and indeed, many aspects of his 'theory' of
history (such as his insistence on the fact that great
events often had trivial causes) merit the adjective
'shallow' which (as I remarked in the opening sentence
of this book) he once applied to himself. Nor was he
(though he certainly wished to be) a great historical
artist, for his histories, like his plays and *contes*, lack
insight into human nature, and his style has neither

116

the polish nor the sonority of that of Gibbon. Yet though he was never to be the Newton or the Darwin of historiography, his contribution to the subject was of immense importance. He inherited the scepticism of 'the Pyrrhonism of history', but instead of using it, as Bayle had done, to compile a 'negative' dictionary of errors, he harnessed it to the task of writing 'positive' history. He was a superb journalist (in the best sense of the term) with an unerring eye for the significant detail and the striking *tableau*. He also had an intuitive grasp of just how much the ordinary reader (to whom, primarily, he addressed himself) was willing to 'take'. And so, although some of his works, and particularly the universal history which he first completed in 1756 and to which he finally gave the name of *Essai sur les mœurs et l'esprit des nations*, find few readers today, their influence at the time was immense. The themes which Voltaire 'plugged' unceasingly, though they were not profoundly original, were nevertheless vitally important. Man and his universe, even if they had remained basically unchanged since the Creation (for Voltaire believed in this event and was no ally of the evolutionists), must have existed for countless centuries; only thus could his mastery over nature, or the evolution of his speech be explained. The civilisations with which Christian historians such as Bossuet had concerned themselves almost uniquely – those of the Middle East and Europe – were in all probability latecomers compared with those of India or China. World history had to be rewritten to conform with these new perspectives. More important still, historiography had to be given a new purpose. Voltaire could, on occasions, play the antiquarian game, but most of the time he scoffed at its pointlessness. Why should one seek to know the precise date when one barbarian king had succeeded another, or establish the exact text of some monkish writing which was probably full of lies and spurious miracles anyhow? Political antiquarianism of the type practised by Boulainvilliers seemed an even greater waste of time: 'I advise those who study and argue in this way to say to the sea: There was a time when you were at Aigues-Mortes, Fréjus, Ravenna and

Ferrara: get back there immediately!'

The purpose of studying and writing history, Voltaire insisted, was education: social, political and moral. There was, of course, nothing fundamentally new in this view, and as Voltaire's agile mind was often content to seize on the first available argument, we find him talking, in highly traditional terms, of the political lessons which princes could derive from a reading of his own *History of Charles XII of Sweden*, or asserting, with Bolingbroke, that history is 'philosophy teaching by examples'. What *was* new, or at any rate relatively so, was his insistence that the only worthwhile type of history was the one which he called 'l'histoire de l'esprit humain', and which we can probably best translate as 'the history of civilisation'. In theory, this meant the history of arts, sciences, inventions, social institutions, 'civilised' modes of behaviour; in short of all the positive achievements on which 'enlightened' man placed most emphasis. It meant too, since these achievements were those of peaceful progress, that history was no longer to be written for the 'instruction' of Machiavellian monarchs, but for the education of all thinking mankind.

In practice, Voltaire achieved less than he promised. To begin with, he was a man in a hurry, and could not always find time to discover the new material he needed. Secondly, he was too narrowly 'modern' in his philosophical outlook, and too 'classical' in his views on art, to achieve a sympathetic insight into many aspects of the more distant past. Thirdly (though in a propagandist this may be considered a strength rather than a weakness), he was just as concerned with denouncing the 'stupidities', 'barbarities' and 'horrors' of the human story as with extolling its more noble aspects. Yet for all this, he probably did as much to create modern historiography as did many of the more speculative historians of later generations. Most contemporaries thought he had achieved a revolution. Certainly Diderot did. 'Other historians,' he wrote, 'relate facts in order to teach us facts. You do so in order to stir up, in the depths of our souls, a profound sense of indignation against lying, ignorance, hypocrisy, superstition, fanaticism and tyranny.'

So far, I have mentioned Diderot only in passing, but it is to him that I shall devote the rest of this chapter: both to the young man whose intellectual pilgrimage, from the Church of which he nearly became a priest to the camp of scientific materialism, reflects, within the compass of a single mind, so many of the developments I have been discussing, and to the mature thinker whose writings, though they often remained unpublished until after his death, contain much of what is most profound in Enlightenment thought. There is also a third Diderot, who is probably better known than either of these: the editor of the *Encyclopédie*; but I shall leave consideration of this work to the next chapter.

Diderot, to my mind, is the greatest of the *philosophes*. Among his possible rivals for this title, only Voltaire shows the same remarkable range of interests and abilities, coupled with the gifts of a great artist. Yet Voltaire, though probably the more influential of the two, because of his unfailing common sense, his clarity and his ability to share the problems of the average intelligent man of his age, lacked (to quote his own word yet again) depth. Many of the problems with which he wrestled (like that of theodicy) no longer torment most of us. Those raised by Diderot, on the other hand, often remain vital issues to this day.

Denis Diderot was born at Langres in 1713, the son of a reasonably wealthy master-cutler. His studies there and at Paris did not lead, as his family, and apparently he himself, had expected, to a quiet ecclesiastical career. Instead he became, for over a decade, one of the many penniless hack-writers of the capital. Many aspects of his life during these early years remain obscure, but what can be established with some certainty is his early contact with, and adherence to, the ideas of the older generation of French *philosophes* and also to those of their English counterparts. Among the latter, Shaftesbury exercised an important influence, for in 1745 Diderot had been asked to translate the latter's *Inquiry concerning virtue or merit* into French. The third Earl of Shaftesbury, whose *Characteristicks*, published in 1711, included many of his earlier essays (among them the *Inquiry*), was a combination of deist and neo-Platonist whose optimistic emphasis on man's natural virtues foreshadowed the 'moral sense' philosophy to which the Scottish Enlightenment in particular was later to be addicted. The passage of time has not enhanced Shaftesbury's reputation (he was perhaps too nice a man to survive), but his appeal to Diderot appears to have been immediate. This can be understood when we consider that the very word 'virtue' (and still more any concrete manifestation of it) was wont to bring tears to the eyes of the philosopher from Langres even when he had become a rigid determinist and an atheistic materialist. It was very largely under the influence of Shaftesbury that Diderot wrote his first significant work, the *Pensées philosophiques* of 1746, though his reading of the French *philosophes*, and of contemporary scientific literature, also made an important contribution, as too did his experience of the religious fanaticism of the *convulsionnaires* – the Jansenist enthusiasts whose hysteria he had witnessed when he was living in the suburb of Saint-Médard where many of their excesses took place.

According to his daughter, Diderot wrote the *Pensées* during the Easter week-end of 1746, and though this is probably a pious legend, their apparent spontaneity and their lack of obvious form make it almost credible. 'I am writing about God', he began, 'and I reckon on having only a few readers.' He was, in reality, writing about many other things too, and his readers, despite the fact that the *Parlement* of Paris hastened to condemn the anonymously published work to the flames, proved to be numerous; there were many clandestine editions. The *Pensées philosophiques* had an attractive name, for the noun suggested the *Pensées* of Pascal, and the adjective (which, since Voltaire's *Lettres*, had become associated with the irreverent) suggested that religious orthodoxy was not likely to be spared. More important, the work itself had a captivating youthful exuberance about it, and this liveliness of style, though it was to become more controlled, was to remain with Diderot for the rest of his life. Style and subject-matter, moreover, went hand in hand, especially in the opening pages which were devoted to a defence of the passions. Here Diderot was following in the footsteps of Shaftesbury, though he soon went far beyond the restrained enthusiasm of his master. Here, too, he was expressing, in brief but forceful terms, a 'philosophy of life' which he was later to expand and develop. Phrases like 'arid rationalism' are still sometimes used to describe, *en bloc*, the thought of the *philosophes*, and there are, of course, a few cases in which they are appropriate. Yet the vitality, the passion and the imagination which are so characteristic of Diderot, are in themselves sufficient proof of the falsity of such uninformed generalisations. It is true, of course, that with him we are not yet quite in the world of the Romantics: when he uses, as he often does, the first-person pronoun, he can usually be interpreted as meaning: 'I, and those who think as I do'; when Rousseau uses it, he means: 'I, the unique individual, Jean-Jacques.'

A defence of the freedom of the passions leads naturally to an attack on those who wish to stifle them. Without explicitly saying so, Diderot tends to equate Christianity with its more superstitious and ascetic adherents, and the argument of the *Pensées* is concerned with illustrating the pernicious social and moral results of their activities as well as with demonstrating the error of their views. Diderot is writing about men as much as about God. He touches, too, on many of the commonplace themes of theologico-philosophical discussion – the possibility of miracles, the authority of the Bible, etc. – but here he has relatively little new to say. It is in the central portion of his argument – where he is concerned with the problem of God's existence – that he shows most originality. This, however, is not immediately obvious, for at first sight the argument appears confused and even contradictory. Indeed, it is contradictory; it is so because Diderot is already employing, though without clearly telling us so beforehand, the method which is to be typical of so many of his later works: he is turning the argument into a dialogue, or rather a series of dialogues.

Atheist and deist are allowed to confront each other and both are allowed to argue against the superstitious fanatic. This transformation into dialogue, however, is not complete. 'Diderot' himself is still there, guiding the debate and intervening in it in order to emphasise that, whatever the logical conclusion of the argument may be, the deist position is psychologically preferable. It is because of this dual approach that the work is initially confusing. Confusion, indeed, appears worse confounded when, in the concluding thoughts of the book, the author interjects a statement of his unquestioning faith in the Roman Catholic Church. This may well be a mere precaution to disarm the censor, but if so it is hardly a very effective one, for at the very end, 'natural' religion is left in possession of the field. Perhaps it is the first example of an attitude characteristic of many of the later dialogues. Diderot loves to push his ideas (or the clash of ideas) to extremes; yet he has a profound mistrust of systems, a deep-rooted fear of being dogmatic. In the *Supplément au voyage de Bougainville*, for example, having demonstrated the superiority of 'natural' to 'civilised' morality, he ends by asserting that the European should stick to his civilisation. In the *Entretien d'un philosophe avec la Maréchale de****, having refined on Bayle's argument that there is no necessary link between religion and morality, he concludes (much to the relief of the orthodox) that one should, in any case, act as though God existed. He even affirms his own willingness to make a deathbed repentance. I say 'he', yet in these later works one can never be sure that the character entitled 'Diderot', 'moi' or 'le philosophe' is giving full expression to his own viewpoint. In the *Entretien d'un père avec enfants*, which debates the very living issue of when (if ever) one should set one's own conscience above the law, Diderot is probably just as much 'mon père' as he is 'moi'. The supreme example of this *dédoublement* is to be found in his greatest literary masterpiece, *Le Neveu de Rameau*. This takes the form of a dialogue between Diderot himself and the dissolute, drifting and cynical nephew of the great musician. The confrontation looks as though it ought to be clear-cut; yet as the argument proceeds, we realise that it will reach no clear moral conclusion, and that Diderot is, in reality, both the 'moi' and the 'lui' of the debate, which becomes an exploration of, rather than a pronouncement on, his (and man's) moral nature and problems. This constant dialectical see-sawing, this refusal to commit himself to a thesis, stem from Diderot's awareness of the complexity (and often the insolubility) of the problems he discusses. They make him probably the most exciting and thought-provoking of the *philosophes*. They also explain, perhaps, why he has rarely been regarded as a great philosopher. His thought was too 'open', too fluid and too spontaneous to provide any sort of finalised *corpus* of philosophical doctrine. The nineteenth century often failed to take it seriously, and, in any case, Victorian susceptibilities were offended by his sexual frankness and his obvious liking for bawdry. It is only in more recent years – and more particularly among philosophers of science – that the profundity of his thought has received fuller recognition.

It has needed a long digression to put us into a position to appreciate the construction of the *Pensées philosophiques*. To appreciate the logic of his argument, a certain reordering of the 'thoughts' themselves is also necessary. It is worth undertaking, however, for the central theme of the *Pensées* – the debate between atheist and deist – constitutes the starting-point of Diderot's odyssey. To begin with, the debate follows a well-worn track. The ontological argument for God's existence and the 'subtle reasonings of the Schoolmen' (among whom, in this context, Diderot places both Descartes and Malebranche) prove, as one might expect, powerless against the defences of the thoroughgoing materialist. Like many others, Diderot's deist turns to science for more convincing demonstrations of divine providence. 'It is only in the works of Newton, of Musschenbroek, of Hartzoeker and of Nieuwentyt,' he writes, 'that satisfactory proofs of the existence of a sovereignly intelligent Being have been found.' The list of names is an interesting one, for Newton, if he still has pride of place, has to share the honours with three relatively unknown men, of whom two are 'life' rather than 'physical' scientists. The reason for Newton's demotion from the pinnacle on which Pope had placed him soon becomes obvious. The atheist has an answer to the 'Newtonian' proof of the existence of God. If we grant that motion is inherent in matter, and if we are given an infinity of time, then it is possible for an organised universe such as the one we know to have developed without guidance from a creative intelligence. With an infinite number of throws of the dice, one will sooner or later get nothing but aces. To this argument, Diderot is unable to reply, though it will probably not convince the reader any more than it did Voltaire, who retorted that Diderot's dice were loaded and that, if you threw a handful of sand for infinity, you would still end up with a handful of sand. Yet behind Diderot's doubts, we can perhaps discern a more serious objection. The Newtonian universe exhibited order, but, as telescopes probed further into space, the purpose of this order became harder to discern. Microscopes, on the other hand, as they revealed the secrets of biology, seemed to discover purpose everywhere. It was the organisation of the worm's eye or the butterfly's wing which really proved the existence of an intelligent creator. For Diderot, the answer to the problems of nature and religion lay henceforth with the biologists.

It did not, however, lie with the deists; or at any rate not for long. For if biology seemed to prove the existence of a creative intelligence, it did not prove that this intelligence was outside, rather than within, nature itself. The pantheism of Spinoza, to which Diderot was soon drawn, fitted the facts equally well. Moreover, by affirming that God *was* Nature, and thus cutting out a link in the universal causal chain, it seemed to have the advantage of simplicity. In the *Promenade du sceptique*, written soon after the *Pensées*, Diderot, whilst maintaining some of the hesitation indicated by the title of the work, gave more weight to the pantheist argument than to any other. Spinoza's influence, moreover, was never to be completely rejected, for Diderot's mature materialism still contained strong elements of vitalism, and a tendency to rhapsodise about Nature (with a capital 'N') remained with him to the end of his days.

However, as he soon saw, there were two faces to biology. Under the microscope, the minutest insect might appear a marvel of purposive creation; yet of a million mayflies, how many escape the swallows and the frost? The birth and growth of a normal child might seem well-nigh miraculous; yet how did two-headed monsters, however rare they might be, square with the hypothesis of an intelligent directing force behind nature? By a change of perspective, 'Nature' could be transformed from a beneficent life-force into what Goethe's Werther was later to call 'an all-devouring and eternally ruminating monster'. If this was so, then, as Diderot was quick to see, the butterfly's wing no longer proved the existence of a divinity. It could itself, moreover, be explained without recourse to such a hypothesis. Life, as Needham appeared to have demonstrated, could generate spontaneously from matter. Among its innumerable possible proliferations (which might all have existed in the beginning) only those which were adapted to their environment would have survived. Like most of his contemporaries, Diderot, at this time, could only see the negative side of evolution. Yet this seemed to him to provide sufficient grounds on which to base a purely materialist explanation of the universe.

The work in which he first expressed his new views was the *Lettre sur les aveugles* of 1749. The question of the relationship between the senses was, as we have seen, central to eighteenth-century epistemology and psychology. On the whole, however, it had been a subject for speculation rather than for experiment. An operation for cataract, on a man blind from birth, might provide vital factual information: when his bandages were first removed, how far would he be able to correlate his new sense with his old ones? The experiment was organised by Réaumur, and Diderot was invited to be present at the critical moment. He soon realised, however, that he had been tricked, and that the bandages had, in fact, already been removed

125

earlier. However, his interest in the problems posed by blindness was now deeply aroused, and the fact that the experiment had turned out to be a 'non-event' did not dissuade him from writing the *Lettres*. He had plenty of other things to say, and, as was frequently the case in his later works, they went far beyond the scope of the original problem. The blind man of Puisaux, whom he went to consult, and the blind mathematician, Saunderson, whose work he read, provided him with valuable information about what the blind imagined sight to be, and about the extent to which they were able to replace their missing sense by developing the potentialities of their existing ones. The meeting with the blind man of Puisaux also led to the introduction of another theme; that of the relativity of moral values. To the blind man, theft (against which he could not guard) seemed the most odious of crimes, and modesty (in dress, at any rate) the most pointless of virtues. Diderot proceeded to argue that a community of men with only four senses (or for that matter one with six) would develop a very different moral code from the one known to us.

If the blind man of Puisaux provided grounds for an attack on the concept of moral absolutes, Saunderson proved less helpful, for his work on algebra did not reveal his intimate thoughts, and since he was already dead, he could not be consulted. However, if he no longer existed, he could at least be invented. Diderot proceeded, therefore, to write his deathbed speech for him, and in it he first gave full expression to his newly developed materialism. To all the arguments of the clergyman, who came to offer him the comforts of religion, Diderot's Saunderson had a ready answer. The stars in their courses, the spectacle of nature, meant nothing to him, since he could not see them. 'If you want me to believe in God, you must make me touch him,' he replied. Adroitly, the clergyman suggested that at least he could touch that miracle of organisation which was his own body. Saunderson, however, could find no proof of God's existence in this more substantial equivalent of the butterfly's wing. It was merely human pride, he argued, which led us to assert,
126

when we failed to understand something ourselves, that it must be the work of God. To do so, moreover, was not to explain the difficulties, but to add to them. 'If nature offers us a knot which is difficult to untie, let us not cut it by making use of a Being, who then becomes for us an even more inextricable knot than the first one.'

The clergyman had one last card to play. He appealed to the example, and the arguments, of those great men who, like Newton, have been convinced that the architecture of the universe presupposed a divine architect. Saunderson conceded that it might, if we considered only this moment of time. However, he proceeded to describe his own idea of a very different world: the world of evolution. The world now presented a spectacle of order only because the beings which once existed, but proved ill-adapted to this order, had become extinct. Perhaps there was once a whole race of men blind like himself; perhaps whole worlds had perished in a similar way. Time, which we could neither define nor understand, transformed everything.

In his dying moments, Saunderson asked the God of Clarke and of Newton to take pity on him. Was this a mere sop to the censor? Probably; but if so it proved an ineffective one. Diderot had not only offended the Church by his arguments, he had also, in his opening remarks, offended a well-connected lady who had been the real first witness of the success of the cataract operation. In addition, he had been rash enough to publish his work at a time of considerable political and religious unrest, when the Government was busily engaged in silencing criticism. As a result, he soon found himself a prisoner in the keep of the fortress of Vincennes.

As he was later to prove, Diderot did not lack courage. Yet he had no taste for martyrdom either, and soon made a number of confessions, together with promises of future good behaviour. These secured his release from close confinement, and he was soon to be freed altogether, largely as a result of the representations of the publishers who had recently commissioned him to edit the *Encyclopédie*.

To this enterprise he was to devote most of his efforts during the next twenty years. Yet he also wrote much else: novels, plays, art criticism, moral, philosophical and scientific essays and dialogues. Where he could do so without jeopardising his own freedom and the safety of the *Encyclopédie*, he published them, as he did his moralising (though unsuccessful) plays and his far more influential writings on dramatic theory. When a work appeared likely to provoke a hostile reaction from religious or political authority, however, he kept it safely under lock and key. On the whole, he erred on the side of caution, and so the majority of his major works did not see the light of day until after his death.

The vitality, the exuberance, the intensity of speculative imagination seen in Diderot's early works, are even more characteristic of many of his later ones. His literary craftsmanship, moreover, has been perfected, and if there are obscurities in the later works (as there are, for example, in *Le Rêve de d'Alembert*) they are usually intentional. In particular, he has mastered the technique of the dialogue, and most of his writings are either avowedly *Entretiens*, or, like *Jacques le fataliste* and the *Supplément au voyage de Bougainville*, tend in practice to become such. The dialogue form gave him the freedom which, as a great artist, he needed. It allowed him to present his philosophical and moral hypotheses in their most extreme form – or sometimes in two opposing extreme forms – without committing himself. And on many matters he did not wish to commit himself, for if ever there was a writer who felt that every thesis had its antithesis, it was he.

Among the many problems with which he wrestled, the most important was probably that posed by the clash between his belief in scientific determinism and his deep sense of moral values and moral responsibility. He could, of course, shock the conventional moral standards of his age; indeed, he frequently delighted in doing so. The suggestion, in the *Lettre sur les aveugles*, that man's concepts of vice and virtue were dependent on his senses, was transformed, in the *Supplément au voyage de Bougainville*, into a demonstration of the

128

way in which they could be determined by the structure and purposes of society. A primitive communism, which aimed at a maximum growth of population, such as that which Bougainville had discovered in Tahiti, produced a totally different ethic (above all, in matters of sexual relationships) from that of property-owning, Christian Western Europe. It also, as the dialogues between Tahitian and European make clear, produced what Diderot regarded as a much better one. Yet this, one of the greatest of the works in praise of the State of Nature, ended with the warning that 'we' should not try to imitate the Tahitians. For we too, if as individuals we were in some sense morally free (or at least felt so), were also conditioned by our environment. The dilemma of the enthusiastic moralist who was also a confirmed determinist haunted Diderot. 'I am furious,' he wrote to Sophie Volland, 'at finding myself bogged down in an accursed philosophy, which my mind is forced to approve of, and my heart forced to contradict.' These words, however, should not be taken – as they sometimes are by logically minded French Cartesian critics – for an admission of total defeat. They were, after all, part of the argument of a love-letter, which then went on to affirm that the mutual love of Denis and Sophie transcended material obstacles; they should be seen in their context. Of course Diderot did 'fail', in so far as he was unable to demonstrate a logical relationship between 'is' and 'ought'. But here he is in good company, and his open admission of failure is preferable to many a spurious success.

Evolutionary materialism was already the creed of the blind Saunderson of the *Lettre sur les aveugles*. It was developed further in the *Pensées sur l'interprétation de la nature*, which Diderot published in 1754, and found its fullest expression in three works which really form a single whole: the *Entretien entre d'Alembert et Diderot*, *Le Rêve de d'Alembert* and the *Suite de l'Entretien*. They were written, probably, in 1769, but not published until the nineteenth century. Diderot suppressed them partly at the insistence of the people portrayed in them, but also, no doubt, because

129

he thought them too daring (in both the philosophical and the sexual senses of the word) for the censorship of the day. He himself summed them up by saying that it was impossible to be, at one and the same time, more profound and more crazy. There is certainly a crazy element in the feverish dreams of d'Alembert, who embroidered on his earlier conversation with Diderot, whilst his mistress, Julie de l'Epinasse, and the hastily summoned Dr Bordeu listen, comment and take notes. Yet in his disconnected fantasies, as in the relatively sane discussions which precede and follow them, there is also a great deal of profundity. By no means all of Diderot's speculations have passed into the corpus of modern science; but enough have done so to make this into one of the high-water marks of eighteenth-century thought.

With the first *Entretien*, we are on relatively solid ground. Here is Diderot the materialist trying to get d'Alembert the deist to admit what the former has been arguing ever since he penned Saunderson's dying speech: that to explain the inexplicable by means of the even more inexplicable is merely to multiply your difficulties. The inexplicable, in this case, is the phenomenon of life. Yet perhaps it can be explained after all, if one is prepared to accept a hypothesis which, though not demonstrable, is also not unreasonable. This hypothesis is that the capacity for sensation is latent in all matter. Like Condillac, Diderot illustrates his thesis by bringing a statue to life, but in a very different way. Ground down into powder, mixed with humus, in which vegetables will grow, the marble of the statue is finally eaten by man. The particles of dead matter have become parts of a living being; their latent sensitivity has become actual. To this hypothesis, to which d'Alembert, needless to say, can make some cogent objections, Diderot quickly adds his comparison between man and machine. In some ways, man reacts to stimuli just as a musical instrument does; if one note is struck, vibrations are set up in others. If the harpsichord could only reproduce itself, it would possess the attributes of life. These attributes are, in a sense, possessed by an egg, yet, in another sense, the egg

130

is still 'dead' matter. All these arguments and analogies may be inconclusive in themselves; but at least they point to the possibility that life is no more than a peculiarly organised form of matter.

It is after this discussion that 'd'Alembert' retires to his fitful slumbers. I shall not attempt to catalogue his dreams, or to list the comments of the man and woman who are listening to them. 'D'Alembert' (and Diderot) range far afield. Yet in their wanderings they discuss vital topics. How is life organised? A swarm of bees can give the impression of continuity; yet in reality the bees are only contiguous. Trembley's polyps are continuous, yet they can divide in almost bee-like fashion. Human life is a continuous organism, yet, as Diderot suggests in an intuition that goes beyond La Mettrie's 'muscular irritability' towards an appreciation of the cellular structure of human tissue, there is also a sense in which it is contiguous. As for the origin of life, Diderot still believed in what the dreaming d'Alembert calls 'the eel-man' (i.e. Needham), and in spontaneous generation. Yet he could also, if only in a brief phrase, suggest something much closer to Lamarck or Darwin. 'The more senses one has, the more needs one has,' says 'd'Alembert', speculating on what it might have been like to be a superior being born on Saturn like one of the heroes of Voltaire's *Micromégas*. 'He is right,' says Bordeu. 'Organs produce needs, and reciprocally, needs produce organs.'

Equally significant, and more audacious, are some of the moral views expressed in the work. Sexual deviations, like auto-erotism or homosexuality (neither of which normally entered into the eighteenth century's scheme of 'tolerance'), are explained as natural phenomena, and the former is almost approved of. Even the idea of 'virtue' (a word so often found on Diderot's own lips) is rejected by 'Bordeu': 'It must be changed into that of doing good, and its opposite into that of doing harm. Either one is happily born, or one is unhappily born; everyone is dragged along irresistibly by the general current, which leads some to glory and others to ignominy.'

These are but snatches from Diderot's argument.

131

They barely begin to illustrate its complexity and 'density'. Indeed, in a short study it is impossible to do so; for this is one of the richest masterpieces of 'philosophic' thought.

7 The Philosophic Crusade

The decade which centred on the year 1750 was the golden age of the *philosophes*. It saw the publication of *De l'Esprit des lois*, of Condillac's major works, of *L'Homme machine*, of the *Lettre sur les aveugles*, of the first volumes of *Encyclopédie* and Buffon's *Histoire naturelle*, of Voltaire's *Histoire universelle*. Turgot's Sorbonne *Discours* of 1750 laid the foundations of the theory of progress, and Rousseau's first two *Discours* (1750 and 1755) already contained the essence of his mature thought. The list could be extended, but it is already long enough to show that, by 1755, the main positions of the French Enlightenment were clearly established. It is true that Helvétius, d'Holbach and Condorcet were still to come; that Voltaire and Rousseau had still to produce the works by which they are best remembered; that the economic theories of the physiocrats (which I cannot attempt to discuss within the compass of this book) had yet to be elaborated. It is true also that many minor figures (such as Mably or Raynal) had still to produce their individual (and sometimes influential) interpretations of the 'philosophical' ideal. Yet by 1755, the great period of discovery was over. The tasks which remained were those of co-ordinating the newly found truths into more systematic bodies of doctrine, of disseminating them among all educated men, and of setting them to work in order to achieve the practical amelioration of society.

Until about the middle of the century, the *philosophes*, despite the close bonds which united many of them, did not form a coherent group or support a common programme. After 1750, though many things continued to divide them, they became what Peter Gay has called 'the Party of Humanity'. They began to take part in collective enterprises, of which the greatest was

133

the *Encyclopédie* itself, but which also included the later *Encyclopédie méthodique*, and the stream of books which issued from the 'propaganda factory' run by d'Holbach. They began to form organised 'pressure groups' within the academies and elsewhere, and to support each other's attempts to gain entry or promotion; Voltaire, for example, made strenuous, though unavailing, efforts to get Diderot into the Académie Française. They collaborated in denouncing, not to say vilifying, men like Fréron, the editor of *L'Année littéraire*, or Palissot, the author of the satirical play, *Les Philosophes*, who had attacked or ridiculed them. More laudably, though less consistently (since Helvétius, for example, was left to fight for himself after the condemnation of *De l'Esprit*), they came to each other's defence in times of persecution; when de Prades, and later Marmontel, were attacked by the Sorbonne, Diderot and Voltaire lent them powerful support. Finally, and this was perhaps their most noble achievement, they combined, usually under Voltaire's leadership, in sustained campaigns for the defence of victims of injustice and intolerance, such as Jean Calas.

This assumption of a more active role might seem to be a natural result of their growing strength and their increasing confidence. Yet it is equally possible to argue that it sprang from completely opposite causes. To ask who started hostilities, the *philosophes* or the political and religious authorities, is a 'chicken and egg' question. However, it is certainly true that the *philosophes* were driven together by the increasing hostility of those in power, as well as pulled together by their common ideals. From about 1745 onwards, the Sorbonne and the Government, who had previously been far more concerned with eradicating Jansenism than with the dangers of 'philosophy', began to look on the latter with a good deal more suspicion. In this, if in little else, they had the constant support of the *Parlements*. Diderot's arrest, in 1749, was an indication of the way things were moving. In the same year, both Montesquieu and Buffon were in trouble with the Sorbonne, and Voltaire, after the death of Mme du

Châtelet, felt the time had come to accept the long-standing invitation of Frederick the Great and remove himself to the safety of Berlin. In the same year, d'Argenson, exaggerating somewhat no doubt, was speaking of 'the French Inquisition'. The *dévots*, and more particularly the Jesuits, were becoming increasingly powerful at court, and though they were later to be held in check by the influence of Mme de Pompadour and her allies, they remained a dangerous threat to the *philosophes*.

If these events played a significant part in bringing about the unity of the *philosophes*, others had the effect of pushing many of them towards a more radical attitude towards social and political reform. For the greater part of his long 'rule', Cardinal Fleury had succeeded in maintaining a good measure of tranquillity in both external and domestic affairs. In 1737, however, he succeeded in bringing about the disgrace of the man who threatened to succeed him, Chauvelin, and he subsequently became more authoritarian and ultramontane in his religious policies. Then, in 1741, he allowed himself to be pushed into war. The War of the Austrian Succession ended in 1748 with the Treaty of Aix-la-Chapelle, but France, despite the victory of Fontenoy, gained little from it. The Government was left with a financial crisis on its hands, which Machault, the finance minister, tried to solve by introducing a new tax. The *vingtième*, as it was called, was to be a tax on income, and was to be paid by all the orders of society. There was an immediate outcry from the nobility, the *Parlements* and the clergy. The last of these, claiming their ancient prerogative of freedom from all taxation, took the lead. Faced with this opposition, undermined by enemies within the Government, and lacking any positive support from the King, Machault was forced to withdraw his proposals, and soon resigned. The same pattern of events was to be repeated more than once before 1789, and the continuing financial crisis was to constitute, if not the main cause, at any rate the principal occasion, of the Revolution itself.

Machault had his champions among the *philo-*

sophes; Voltaire was outstanding among them. Yet the majority were not particularly concerned, for they were not 'politicians'. It was only gradually, when the Seven Years War brought new military and economic disasters, and the rift between aristocratic *Parlements* and reforming ministers of the Crown widened, that the need for some sort of major political and social change became apparent, and more and more *philosophes* began to devote their attention to the problem of the form this change should take. Even then, the 'philosophic' party never became a 'party' in the modern sense of the term. The policies they advocated were as varied as they were numerous. The idea (popular in the early nineteenth century) that they were a band of democratic revolutionaries can be quickly dismissed. Democracy was advocated only by a small minority, among whom Rousseau is the most important figure, and even then it was hedged about with all sorts of restrictions. 'Revolution', though it came increasingly to be regarded as a possibility, was not advocated as a practical policy. On the contrary, a majority of the reformers took a relatively authoritarian line. Change was needed, but it should come from above, not from the fickle populace. There were deep divisions, however, as to just how much change was needed, and as to what was meant by 'above'. Voltaire, pragmatic as ever, thought that the main aim was to restrict the power of the Church and reduce (though not abolish) the privileges of the aristocracy, and that the best man to do the job (in France at any rate) would be an 'enlightened' despot. Helvétius, on the other hand, dreamed of a supreme authority which would initiate a far more radical programme of change: the key to the future happiness of mankind lay, he believed, in education, for, as Condillac had shown, man was a product of his experiences. It also lay, since Helvétius was the first thoroughgoing utilitarian, in an appreciation of the fact that the aim of political activity was the greatest happiness of the greatest number. However, as the 'greatest number' had not grasped this themselves, they must be led to happiness by some more prescient authority. If sensationalism, since it

136

affirmed that all men were endowed with identical natural qualities, would seem to have democratic implications, these were certainly not visible in *De l'Esprit*, for its author coupled a 'Rousseauist' admiration for the virtues of totalitarian Sparta with a 'pre-Romantic' belief in the almost transcendental importance of the man of genius. Even d'Holbach, who delighted in calling upon men to throw off the combined yoke of priests and kings, was careful to make it clear that he was not urging the populace to revolt; the revolution he desired was basically technocratic rather than democratic. Similar views were expressed by utopian socialists such as Morelly and Mably.

Nevertheless, their denunciations of existing authority, together with the attacks on tyranny, slavery and colonialism which were to be found in Raynal's immensely popular *Histoire philosophique des établissements et du commerce des Européens dans les deux Indes*, of 1772, resulted in the creation of a considerable body of public opinion which felt dissatisfied with things as they were. When the aged, and by now predominantly conservative, Voltaire could suggest that perhaps the only just war was that of Spartacus, when the greatest comic dramatist of the age could draw applause by getting Figaro to say to his aristocratic master: 'You took the trouble to be born, nothing more,' then, with a little imagination and a lot of hindsight, it is easy to hear the tumbrils rumbling in the distance.

The question whether, and if so how far, the Enlightenment may be considered a 'cause' of the Revolution, has been debated endlessly and largely fruitlessly. However, at the extremes of the debate, two points at least can be fairly firmly established. Firstly, despite the arguments of the abbé Barruel and his long progeny, the Revolution was in no sense a 'philosophic', 'Encyclopedic' or 'Masonic' plot. Secondly, the creation of the National Assembly, and the legislation enacted by it and its successors, were deeply indebted to 'philosophic' thought. To attempt to go beyond such general conclusions is to involve oneself in another of Diderot's 'chicken and egg' debates, or to indulge in a

137

futile search for a balance in which to weigh, say, the *Encyclopédie* against the price of bread.

I shall, therefore, not attempt to pursue the subject further. Instead, I shall examine more closely three important themes which come within the scope of the Enlightenment itself. If I give pride of place to the *Encyclopédie*, this is not so much because of its 'monumental' qualities as because of the ideals that inspired it and the dramatic struggle which accompanied its publication. My second subject will be the achievement of Voltaire, who, in his last great incarnation as Patriarch of Ferney, dominated his age. Lastly, I shall consider some aspects of the theory of progress, which finds its most complete expression in the work of Condorcet.

Nothing could be more in keeping with the 'enlightened' spirit than the idea of a single work which included all that was most vital and useful in 'modern' knowledge. Chambers' *Cyclopaedia*, published in England in 1728, constituted the first important step in this direction, but it was relatively modest in scope. In 1737 the Scottish Jacobite exile whom the French knew as 'le chevalier Ramsay' suggested to an audience of French Freemasons that they should undertake something on a more ambitious scale. Ramsay, a disciple of Fénelon, had by this time moved closer to a belief in natural religion. He did not, however, suggest that the proposed work should be a direct expression of such views; indeed, he explicitly excluded from it both religion and politics. It is perhaps worth adding that in its early days French Freemasonry possessed few of the anti-clerical attributes it was later to acquire.

The next move was also to be taken by a Freemason, though no clear link between him and Ramsay has ever been established. Early in 1745 the publisher Le Breton agreed to a proposal, by the German scholar Sellius, to publish a translation of Chambers. However, Sellius and his English partner, Mills, soon proved their incompetence, as did their immediate successor, Gua de Malves. Le Breton looked elsewhere; he also sought to ensure fuller commercial backing for the enterprise through an alliance with other publishers; it was one of these who first brought to his notice the man who had recently translated James's *Medical Dictionary*; in 1746, the then almost unknown Diderot was given the task.

If Le Breton had wanted a translator, Diderot had other ideas, which he soon succeeded in imposing. He envisaged a work of far greater scope and originality than 'Chambers', and immediately set about building up a team of collaborators. His efforts to bring in the 'big names' met with only partial success, for though Voltaire promised (and gave) his support, Buffon and Montesquieu remained lukewarm. However, specialists in many fields agreed to contribute, and a nucleus of younger enthusiasts was also soon formed. Among them was Jean-Jacques Rousseau – then, if anything, even more obscure than Diderot – who contributed articles on music. The greatest success of this recruiting campaign, however, was the enlistment of d'Alembert as fellow-editor with particular responsibility for the mathematical articles. The young mathematician was already famous for his *Traité de dynamique*, and his name gave an air of respectability to the work, which Diderot himself, especially after the *Lettre sur les aveugles* and his subsequent imprisonment, was in no position to provide.

In 1750 enough progress had been made for Diderot to publish his *Prospectus*. In it he pointed out the limitations of Chambers and emphasised the importance which the new work was to attach to the history of science, and more particularly to what we now term technology. His views were to be echoed and amplified by d'Alembert's *Discours préliminaire*, which appeared in the first volume of the *Encyclopédie* itself, in July 1751.

Rarely has a work been better launched than by the *Discours*, even though d'Alembert's writing has the mellow confidence of mature burgundy rather than the sparkle of champagne. He was well aware of the reefs on which the new work might founder, and took care not to associate it with anything that smacked of subversion or heresy; Bayle, for example, whose *Dictionnaire* was an obvious ancestor, received no mention.

Instead, d'Alembert struck a proudly patriotic note. Yet at the same time he succeeded in stressing the original qualities of the *Encyclopédie* itself, and also produced one of the most succinct and forceful summaries of 'enlightened' thought to be found anywhere. The opening section explained the origin of knowledge in 'sensationalist' terms, and then proceeded to affirm the essential unity of this knowledge and to analyse its genealogical structure. Here, like Diderot in the *Prospectus* (though even more explicitly), d'Alembert followed in the footsteps of Francis Bacon, whom the Encyclopedists proclaimed as their model, despite the fact that the alphabetical presentation of their own work really precluded them from adopting his thematic plan. Their debts to some more recent thinkers are indicated in the second section of the *Discours*, which is devoted to a sketch of the progress of the arts, sciences and philosophy since the Renaissance. Here, d'Alembert is always clear and often penetrating. He shares, of course, many of the prejudices of his age and of his country. The Middle Ages, for example are quickly dismissed as barbarous, and the Renaissance itself, though eulogised, is treated almost as perfunctorily; whilst French poetry is discussed at some length in terms which differ little from those used in Boileau's *Art poétique* nearly a century earlier, the Italians are hardly mentioned, and the Spanish Golden Age joins the English Elizabethans in oblivion. Yet when he writes about science and philosophy since the time of Bacon and Descartes, d'Alembert is far more judicious. A sense of historical relativism, so clearly lacking in his treatment of the more distant past, characterises much of what he has to say about Descartes, whose greatness, as he clearly shows, should not be denied merely because, in some fields, he has been superseded by Newton and Locke. Even Leibniz, with whom d'Alembert is fundamentally out of sympathy, is treated with considerable respect. More fulsome praise is bestowed, as one might expect, on great contemporaries such as Condillac, Buffon, Maupertuis and Voltaire. There is, however, one significant exception: the author of the *Encyclopédie*'s musical articles had recently achieved notoriety by the *Discours sur les sciences et les arts* in which he questioned the benefits of civilisation. D'Alembert is not unduly disturbed; he can still refer to Rousseau as 'eloquent and philosophical', and reply mildly by pointing to the achievements he has just outlined; however, the first signs of a crack in the united front of the Encyclopedists are beginning to appear. They are not to be the last.

Despite d'Alembert's apparent serenity, and despite the fact that it seemed to crown a great period of intellectual achievement, the *Encyclopédie* appeared at what was, in fact, a very dangerous moment. Increased ecclesiastical watchfulness, together with increased governmental nervousness resulting from the crisis over Machault's proposed reforms, had already landed its editor in gaol. From the beginning (and, from their point of view, justifiably) the Jesuits had been suspicious of the new work. Their *Journal de Trévoux* had accused Diderot's *Prospectus* of plagiarism. After the appearance of the first volume of the *Encyclopédie*, the complaint was renewed, all the more vigorously since their own *Dictionnaire* was being plagiarised. Other complaints were soon added. There was little to attack in aricles like 'Athée', but 'Âme' and 'Autorité politique' were not as orthodox as they might have been, and Diderot's technique (to which the article 'Encyclopédie' later confessed) of slipping his more 'philosophical' comments into articles with inoffensive titles ('Aius locutius', 'Agnus scythicus') did not altogether escape watchful eyes. Pressure on the King to take action led to the imposition of stricter censorship by the Directeur de la Librairie. However, Malesherbes, newly appointed to this post, soon had an opportunity to demonstrate his personal sympathy with the Encyclopedists.

Diderot had certainly taken risks, but these were not sufficiently grave to provoke more serious government action. Some more pressing reason was needed, and the theologians were soon to find one. In November 1751, the abbé de Prades, a contributor to the *Encyclopédie* on religious matters, sustained, to the accompaniment of general applause, his Sorbonne thesis. In the following

ing month the applause turned to abuse, and in January, disgraced and threatened with arrest, the abbé fled to Berlin. Clearly, Church and *Parlement* were now determined to take a more rigorous stand, for the Lockean sensationalism which (together with some leanings towards natural religion) constituted de Prades's 'heresy' had hitherto met with their approval. Clearly, too, they were less interested in suppressing the heresy itself than with attacking the Encyclopedists, for Condillac, the most outstanding of French sensationalists, was left undisturbed.

It was in the midst of this uproar that the second volume of the *Encyclopédie* appeared. It contained the article 'Certitude' by the abbé de Prades, and diligent scrutiny soon revealed that here, too, was heresy. Faced with this evidence, the Government decided to ban further printing and distribution of the work. Diderot's own papers only escaped seizure because the sympathetic Malesherbes hid them in his own house. It was Malesherbes, too, who worked most effectively to procure the lifting of the ban. He was helped by d'Alembert, who was very good at protestations of outraged innocence, and also, very possibly, by Mme de Pompadour, who on the whole favoured the *philosophes* and certainly hated the Jesuits. As a result of their efforts, the *Encyclopédie* was allowed to appear again after three months, though an even more rigid censorship was imposed on it. Three more volumes were published by 1755. New collaborators joined the 'team'. Among them were the chevalier de Jaucourt, who was to prove almost as indefatigable as Diderot himself, and the baron d'Holbach. The latter was already known for his scientific work, though his materialist propaganda was still a thing of the future. His Paris home and country house were soon to become the principal meeting-places of the Encyclopedists.

A new crisis soon developed. It began in January 1757, with Damiens's attempt to assassinate Louis XV. The Government introduced savage laws against 'subversive' literature, and though Damiens had no connections with the *philosophes*, attempts were made to link his deed with their beliefs. Moreau's *Nouveau mémoire pour servir à l'histoire des Cacouacs* was one of the first and most successful of a new wave of 'anti-philosophic' writings. The Encyclopedists themselves were also guilty of tactical errors. D'Alembert's article 'Genève' described with obvious approval how Calvinist pastors were moving towards Socinianism (a type of unitarianism); it also advocated the establishment of a theatre in Geneva. This provoked angry complaints from the Genevan authorities and led Rousseau (increasingly estranged from the *philosophes*) to attack the theatre in his *Lettre à d'Alembert*. For the mathematician, who was touchy, underpaid and increasingly out of sympathy with the materialism of Diderot and d'Holbach, this seemed the last straw. Early in 1758 he told Voltaire of his decision to withdraw from editorship of the *Encyclopédie*. After trying to dissuade him, Voltaire swung round to his point of view and began to put pressure on Diderot to bring the work to a halt or transfer it abroad. Courageously, Diderot refused, and prepared to carry on alone.

The quarrel might have led to total rupture had not other events precipitated a greater crisis. In the summer of 1758 there appeared (anonymously, though with the approval of the French censor) a book entitled *De l'Esprit*. The author's name was an open secret. Claude Adrien Helvétius, a former *fermier-général* and now one of the members of the d'Holbach circle, had been advised by many friends to publish his work abroad or not at all. Relying on the permission of the censor (who was to live to regret it), he had ignored their warnings. His decision was a rash one, for *De l'Esprit*, despite its occasional protestations of orthodoxy, was the first clear statement of the materialist position, which many, friend and foe alike, had sensed to be implicit in sensationalist philosophy. If the pleasure–pain principle explained the behaviour of Condillac's statue when it sniffed a rose or touched a thorn, then it must also explain any tenable theory of ethics. All human activities were rooted in self-love, and the only possible moral system was one which built on this foundation. It could only do so by showing that crime did not pay and that virtue received rich re-

143

wards, and the only logically possible basis for the concepts of 'crime' and 'virtue' was the utilitarian theory (already found in the abbé de Saint-Pierre) of the greatest happiness of the greatest number. If society were properly constructed, and men properly educated, then harmony and progress would ensue. Social reform and education were therefore the twin pillars of Helvétius' argument. He did not, however, make clear who the reformers and educators were to be. Presumably they were to be the men of genius. But, one may inquire, what would happen if the genius turned out to be the marquis de Sade? We can hardly expect Helvétius to answer this question himself, for the marquis was then only eighteen; yet it has obsessed one of the most perspicacious of recent writers on the Enlightenment, Lester Crocker. Perhaps it also obsessed some of the theologians who attacked the work, though to suggest this may be to do them more than justice, since they do not appear to have responded to the humanitarianism so clearly manifest in many of the details of Helvétius' work, like his denunciation of slavery. The outcry against *De l'Esprit* was, in fact, immediate and almost universal, and in August the work was condemned. Its author had to make humiliating retractions, and was probably lucky to suffer no worse punishment.

He received little support from his fellow-*philosophes*. They rightly took the view that he had been warned, and no doubt feared that his indiscretion would endanger them all. In this they proved equally right, for in January 1759 the *Parlement* issued a condemnation of eight subversive works, among which were both *De l'Esprit* and the *Encyclopédie*. The latter escaped the flames, but in March the *Conseil d'État* (the royal Government) intervened once again, revoking the publishers' privilege and forbidding further distribution of the volumes which had already appeared. Subscribers were given the right to demand their money back, and had they done so, the work would have been effectively crippled. No one did, however, and Diderot, who had signed a new contract with the publishers after d'Alembert's final withdrawal

144

from editorship, was able to go ahead with his task. By the end of 1765, the final volumes of the text were ready. They were distributed, as they had been printed, clandestinely. The Government, however, made no attempt to interfere; particularly since the expulsion of the Jesuits in 1764, it had become markedly less hostile. In 1772, with the appearance of the last volumes of plates, the work was completed.

Its influence was powerful. It has been estimated that, if reprints and translations are included, some 20,000 copies were sold. Yet with its seventeen volumes of text and eleven of plates, it was clearly a work that only the wealthy could afford. It was the myth of the *Encyclopédie* that was more widely influential, and this myth was at least as much the creation of its opponents as of its contributors. For whilst it is true that daringly 'philosophical' ideas were sometimes slipped into minor articles, and that a reformist note was sounded in some of the major ones (d'Alembert's 'Collège' and 'Genève', for example) the vast majority of those which dealt with politics and religion kept firmly to the middle of the road. The principal Encyclopedists, though, as their opponents well knew, they would have liked to be 'subversive', were usually too cautious to be so in fact. But for the campaign against it, which told the reader that he ought to be 'shocked' and indicated where he would find the 'shocking' passages, the work would probably have had relatively little effect as propaganda. Even supporters, like Voltaire, felt that so many precautions had been taken and so many concessions made, that it was only a pale reflection of what it ought to have been. They were right, of course, in so far as the *Encyclopédie* was intended as a vehicle of 'reform'; but was this its main aim? Diderot's statements, and his actions, indicate that this was not the case. From the beginning, he stressed the scientific and technological importance of the work, and the care he took over the eleven volumes of plates indicates that his words were no mere camouflage. The 'subversive myth' which grew up around the *Encyclopédie* was a vital part of its influence. The effect of its 'subversive' passages was, however, probably far less important

145

than that of the unobtrusive substitution of a pre-dominantly scientific outlook for the traditional religious one. It is its role in this 'silent revolution' that, in the long run, makes the work a landmark in the history of thought.

Not everyone, however, was prepared to wait for 'the long run'. Among the many who wanted to alter things here and now, the most effective was the mature Voltaire. For many years after the condemnation of the *Lettres philosophiques*, it seemed that he had learnt the error of his ways. He avoided publishing anything on the controversial aspects of politics and religion, and settled down, ostensibly at any rate, to the study of Newtonian physics and to the writing of classical tragedy and didactic poetry. Above all, in the forties, he made strenuous efforts to become a courtier. He even had a measure of success, for the ode with which he celebrated the victory of Fontenoy in 1745 led to his appointment as Royal Historiographer and prepared the way for his entry into the Academy. Louis, however, never trusted him very far, rightly suspecting that his exaggerated obsequiousness hid thoughts of a very different nature. Voltaire, moreover, though he managed to keep his *Traité de métaphysique* and the essays in biblical criticism he had composed with Mme du Châtelet under lock and key, was always taking risks. He published his poem *Le Mondain* ostensibly to celebrate the earthly paradise in which he lived, but also to satirise the one inhabited by Adam and Eve; he published the introduction to his *Siècle de Louis XIV*, which was quickly suppressed; he did *not* publish the obscene poem, *La Pucelle*, in which he satirised the Maid of Orléans, but he had been rather careless with the manuscript copies. Not surprisingly, his period of courtly favour proved brief, and it was in semi-disgrace that he left for Prussia in 1750. Significantly, perhaps, his departure had been preceded by a revival of his interest in politics. He was an enthusiastic supporter of Machault and his *vingtième*, and his pamphlet, *La Voix du sage et du peuple*, aroused opposition which no doubt helped to speed him on his way. In Berlin, breathing what at first seemed to be free air again, he completed his *Siècle de Louis XIV*, and though this was by no means an anti-monarchical work, he struck a more pronouncedly anti-clerical note in the new final chapters. There, too, he began some of the deistic writings which he was only to publish many years later, including the *Dictionnaire philosophique*, his 'one-man' encyclopedia. However, success at Frederick's court proved no more lasting than at Louis's, and by 1753 he was on the move again. 'On the run' might be a more accurate description, for he was arrested in Frankfurt by Frederick's minions, and later, finding that he was *persona non grata* in Paris, he tried vainly to discover a refuge in southern France. It was not until 1755 that he came to rest at 'Les Délices' in Geneva. Three years later, he bought the château of Ferney, just across the border in France. He came there, an old man, to cultivate his garden and to die. However, he did not achieve the latter aim until 1778, and meanwhile he was to live through the most glorious period of his career.

He had not been inactive during the years of wandering, but he had done his best to avoid trouble. Even after he reached the haven of Geneva, he still showed a good deal of caution. The *Poème sur le désastre de Lisbonne*, though hardly 'Christian' in its message, avoided any direct provocation of the Church. The *Histoire universelle*, especially in the version of 1756, was moderate in tone, even though it managed to antagonise the pastors by its condemnation of Calvin's 'judicial murder' of Servetus. If there was any subject on which Voltaire was almost prepared to go to war with the Genevan authorities, it was the (to us) relatively trivial one of the establishment of a theatre at 'Les Délices'.

'Il faut cultiver notre jardin'; the most famous of all Voltaire quotations was not the battle-cry of a reformer. The positive message of *Candide*, in so far as it had one, was that one should withdraw from an evil world, gather one's close friends about one, and try to construct a little haven of peace. At least, this is what the text *says*, and, to judge from his correspondence at

147

the time, what Voltaire himself thought. Yet those who have interpreted it otherwise have at least had the right intuitions, for they have sensed that a man capable of writing this furious onslaught on human folly would not be content to settle down to gardening. Soon after completing *Candide*, Voltaire moved to Ferney, and his tone rapidly began to change. The reforming Voltaire of the *Lettres philosophiques* had long been partially eclipsed by the ambitious courtier and the despondent exile. The Patriarch of Ferney soon set about making up for lost time.

'Écrasez l'infâme'; the slogan appears to have been invented by Frederick the Great, but Voltaire was soon to make it his own. He never defined the 'infamous thing' that had to be crushed, yet, though it could include almost any manifestation of superstition, intolerance, cruelty or just plain stupidity, it meant, more often than not, the Roman Catholic Church. For years, Voltaire had been persecuted by Jansenist and Jesuit alike. Now, rich, remote and with a convenient border to escape over should he not prove remote enough, he began to strike back. 'Let us work in the Lord's vineyard,' he wrote to all his friends, and 'the Lord', in this case, was that rather unlikely figure, a deist God of wrath, come to avenge his slaughtered saints. Many years ago, as a young exile, Voltaire had read the English deists; at Cirey, he and Mme du Châtelet had spent their time tearing to bits Dom Calmet's absurd commentary on the Bible; he had witnessed the convulsions of the fanatics of Saint-Médard and seen the Church defeat the reforms by which Machault might have saved the French monarchy. For the most part, his reactions had been consigned to his notebooks and to his memory. In Berlin, he had begun the job of sorting them out, but only now did he set about publishing them to the world.

It was a crucial moment. As Voltaire was settling in at Ferney, the *Parlement* was condemning the *Encyclopédie*, *De l'Esprit* and six other works. Moreau's attack on the 'Cacouacs' had been followed by many others, among them Abraham Chaumeix's *Préjugés légitimes contre l'Encyclopédie*. 1760 saw the production of

Palissot's play, *Les Philosophes*, a crude and not very funny satire. A little later, Le Franc de Pompignan celebrated his election to the Academy by an inaugural speech which attacked the 'philosophical' sect. The campaign against the Encyclopedists seemed to be working towards a climax; the 'French Inquisition', of which the marquis d'Argenson had spoken, might yet become as established as its Spanish counterpart.

Voltaire could have stood aside. He was, after all, a great poet whose youthful indiscretions could be forgiven. Though he had been an Encyclopedist, the articles he had contributed were on innocuous subjects, and he certainly did not belong, either physically or spiritually, to the atheistic d'Holbach circle. Palissot, who knew him, had been careful not to include him in the satire of *Les Philosophes*. For his part, he took equal care not to attack Palissot, for he knew that the dramatist was the indirect protégé of the new all-powerful minister, the duc de Choiseul. Voltaire had high hopes of Choiseul, as he so often had of those in authority. Yet though he compromised on Palissot, fundamentally his die was cast.

With the energy of a man forty years younger, he threw himself into the struggle. To this day, there are important aspects of the 'order of battle' of this one-man army which have never been elucidated. Did he arrange for some of his works to be published almost simultaneously in four or five different places, or was it just that publishers throughout Europe were phenomenally quick at reprinting everything he wrote? If we cannot answer this question with assurance, we can at least identify some of the weapons he used. In 1760 Abraham Chaumeix was destroyed by a bomb entitled *Le Pauvre Diable*, whilst Le Franc de Pompignan fell victim to a new weapon, which might be described as a pamphlet machine-gun, for it rattled off a series of bursts of fire with names such as Les 'Quand', Les 'Si' and Les 'Pourquoi'. Voltaire's ridicule was usually lethal, and never more so than in these short pamphlets, dozens of which were soon to follow.

The heavier weapons were soon brought into action. One of the first, and one of the most deadly, was the

149

Sermon des cinquante, which had probably been in the armoury for some time, but was published in 1762. Of all Voltaire's attacks on Christianity, this was perhaps the most concentrated and the most bitter. Today, it may seem prejudiced and totally lacking in a sense of historical relativism, for Voltaire, following in the footsteps of Bayle and English deists such as Tindal, judges the Bible from the moral standpoint of an enlightened eighteenth-century liberal, and not surprisingly finds it barbarous. Yet to criticise him on these grounds (as Renan and many others were to do in the following century) is to show a precisely similar lack of relativism. Voltaire must be judged in the context of eighteenth-century Christianity, and, by and large, the eighteenth-century Church maintained that the Bible contained both literal truth and absolute morality. In his presentation of details, Voltaire could, and often did, cheat. Yet fundamentally his indignation was utterly sincere and, again in the context of his times, largely justified.

In the years that followed, the same arguments were to be repeated, in a way which even a sympathetic modern reader is tempted to describe as 'ad nauseam'. Among the many works which contain them (and which I shall not even begin to list) were the *Dictionnaire philosophique portatif* (first published in 1764, and rapidly expanded in later editions) and *La Philosophie de l'histoire* (published in 1765 and later incorporated into the *Essai sur les mœurs*). The *Dictionnaire philosophique* contains much of what Voltaire looked for (and failed to find) in the *Encyclopédie*. The political, social, and above all religious criticism, which the Encyclopedists had had to suppress or tuck away in obscure corners, is here given pride of place. *La Philosophie de l'histoire*, whilst containing much that is positive, has a lengthy section devoted to yet another demonstration of the iniquity of the Old Testament Jews.

The campaign continued to the end of Voltaire's life, but it underwent significant modification. The works mentioned above, and others published about the same time, such as the *Examen important de Mi-*

lord Bolingbroke, had probably been written, or at least started, at Cirey or Potsdam. At this time, Voltaire's hostility to Christianity included the person of its founder. Later, however, he made an increasingly important distinction between the religion of the gospels (which he could admire) and the barbarities and adsurdities common to Judaism and the institutionalised Church. He may well have done so, in part, for tactical reasons. In 1766, a new edition of d'Holbach's *Le Christianisme dévoilé* marked the beginning of a parallel anti-Christian offensive by the atheist wing of the Encyclopedists. Voltaire, however, did not welcome his new allies. His deism was probably sincere, and in any case he was convinced that d'Holbach's extremism was rocking the 'philosophic' boat. For a time, his campaign became a war on two fronts, and indeed the *Histoire de Jenni* of 1775 shows him more preoccupied with refuting the atheists than with ridiculing the Church. His concern for the unity of the movement, however, soon led him to abandon his anti-atheist polemics. A similar desire to broaden the struggle against *l'infâme* may explain his new-found liking for the simple religion of Jesus; a door was left open by which even Christians (a few of them at least) might enter the heavenly city of 'philosophy'.

Most of these works, of course, were published clandestinely and anonymously, but it was usually fairly easy to identify their author, whose words were always eagerly read, even by those who did not share his views. As the small pamphlet could usually escape police control, Voltaire could reach a far wider audience than a work like the *Encyclopédie*. In his defence of the 'philosophic' cause, he was, of course, helped by events. The *Parlement*'s condemnation of the Jesuits, and their subsequent expulsion by the Government, did much to relieve the pressure on the new ideas. Yet his own contribution was outstanding.

It would have been less so if he had confined himself to attacking the history and doctrines of the Church. However, he combined these attacks with a vigorous defence of contemporary victims of intolerance and injustice, and in so doing became the symbolic champion

151

of the cause of humanity. When at last, on the eve of his death, he returned in triumph to Paris, he was, it is said, greeted by the populace as 'l'homme aux Calas'; it was his vindication of the memory of an innocent man broken on the wheel and the aid he had given to the victim's family which had made the deepest impression on the public mind. Calas, a Huguenot merchant in the intolerantly Catholic city of Toulouse, had been executed in 1762, allegedly for murdering his son, who had wanted to become a Catholic. It took three years of constant campaigning to force the Government to quash the court's verdict, and Voltaire's role was throughout the dominant one. Moreover, the Calas case was to be only the first of many. Before it was over, Voltaire was already undertaking the defence of Sirven, accused of a somewhat similar crime, and it was not until 1771 that he was finally successful. Meanwhile, in 1766, the chevalier de La Barre had been barbarously executed for a number of relatively trivial acts of impiety. This time, the victim was a *libertin*, who had been reading the *Dictionnaire philosophique* (his copy of it was burnt along with his body), and Voltaire, feeling the threat to himself and his friends, reacted with even greater vigour. His interventions, moreover, were not restricted to cases where religious persecution was involved. Even in his Geneva days, he had made efforts to save Admiral Byng, shot on his own quarter-deck 'to encourage the others'. Now, he took up the case of the comte de Lally, the former French commander in India who, in 1766, had suffered a somewhat similar fate. His efforts on Lally's behalf were to continue to the end of his life.

Meanwhile, Voltaire had not been inactive in the fields of politics and social reform. As the gap between Government and *Parlement* steadily widened, he identified himself more and more with the cause of royal authority. His grievances against the *Parlement* were of long standing, and were reinforced by the La Barre and Lally cases. His *Histoire du Parlement de Paris* of 1769, written, almost certainly, with some degree of ministerial backing, disputed many of the claims of that institution; in later editions, the tone became even more critical. When the *Parlements* were dissolved by Maupeou in 1771, Voltaire applauded wholeheartedly. The King's ministers, on the other hand, usually had his support. He courted Choiseul assiduously, even though the latter went some way towards conciliating the *Parlements*. However, it was when Turgot became Controller-General and attempted to introduce much-needed reforms that his enthusiasm was really aroused. The sight of a *philosophe* in power seemed like a presage of the millennium. When the bread riots of 1775 began to threaten Turgot's position, Voltaire wrote strongly in his support, and when the minister was dismissed in 1776, the Patriarch of Ferney suffered a blow from which he was never to recover (in the political sense at least) before his own death two years later.

Yet though he was a 'royalist' at home and a somewhat naïve admirer of 'enlightened' despots abroad (Frederick and Catherine in particular), he could also, faced with a different political situation, adopt an almost democratic position. Among Geneva's ruling oligarchy, he had many friends. Yet when the position of this oligarchy was challenged by successive waves of popular opinion, Voltaire not only allowed himself to be drawn into the dispute, but gave his support to the agitators. In Geneva, the machinery for middle-class participation in the Government existed; it was therefore right to try to use it. In politics, Voltaire was above all a pragmatist; different situations demanded different remedies.

What really mattered to Voltaire was not who governed, but how they governed. In numerous articles in the *Dictionnaire philosophique* and the *Questions sur l'Encyclopédie*, in his *Commentaire* on Beccaria's humanitarian proposals for judicial and penal reform, and in many other places, he defines the ideals at which any government should aim: the abolition of the remnants of feudalism; restriction of the civil power of the Church; the provision of education for all those (this did not include the peasantry) who could benefit from it; the abolition of legal torture and of barbarous punishments; the establishment of the right to pro-

153

perty and of liberty within the law. The list could be lengthened indefinitely, for in Voltaire's political writings one finds a whole programme of bourgeois liberal reforms. Some, like the ending of the official persecution of the Protestants, or of *lettres de cachet*, were to be brought about by the Old Regime itself; others were to be introduced at the time of the Revolution; many more are still unachieved in large areas of the modern world. This is one reason why Voltaire still has his significance for the twentieth century.

The idea of progress can be traced back a long way; certainly to the time of Fontenelle and the Quarrel of the Ancients and Moderns, probably back to Descartes and Bacon, and very possibly to the Renaissance. In the eighteenth century, as I have tried to show, an awareness of the reality of progress and the need for progress underlies a great deal of 'Enlightenment' thought. Yet such an awareness does not, in the majority of cases, constitute a theory of progress. The cyclical theory of history, which was, like most things, as old as Plato, still held powerful sway over many of the *philosophes*. They were, it is true, unwilling to accept its empire. Montesquieu, aware of the possibility of an endless alternation between despotism and anarchy, sought to achieve a measure of stability through an elaborate system of social checks and balances; Voltaire, having descried a few gleams of light in centuries of stupidity and horror, tried to keep the flame alive, but kept emphasising the ease with which it could be extinguished. The Encyclopedists gave similar warnings. 'Barbarism,' said d'Alembert in the *Discours préliminaire,* 'lasts for centuries, and seems to be our natural element; reason and good taste are merely transient.' Diderot held similar views, and the article 'Progrès', which is very possibly by him, is one of the shortest and most non-committal in the whole work.

Rousseau enthused over progress in the opening paragraphs of his *Discours sur les arts et les sciences*, which glorified man's achievement since the Renaissance. In the *Discours sur l'inégalité*, he described the early development of the human race, and showed it to

154

be the inevitable result of 'la faculté de se perfectionner'. In *Du Contrat social*, he produced what later generations were to regard as a blueprint for the future progress of society. Yet, 'progressive' though he was, Rousseau presented his ideas in an intellectual framework which was totally hostile to the idea of progress. The two *Discours* both went on to prove that 'progress' had meant decay and degeneration, rather than advance. The establishment of the 'social contract' state did not appear as a 'great leap forward' which future societies might yet make, but as something that had happened in the past. A society based on the rule of the general will could be preserved for a while by various political devices derived from the practice of classical antiquity, but, sooner or later, it would inevitably founder.

All this serves to emphasise the originality of the twenty-three-year-old ecclesiastic who, in 1750, was entrusted with the task of delivering, in Latin, the opening and closing speeches of the annual academic exercises of the Sorbonne. Anne Robert Jacques Turgot was soon to leave the Church for the magistrature, and was to play an important role in his country's political history. In the history of thought, however, this was to prove his greatest moment. He was fortunate, perhaps, to be able to deliver his lectures the year before the abbé de Prades sustained his ill-fated thesis. For though he was speaking in praise of Christianity, what he succeeded in demonstrating was not so much the contribution of the Christian Church to human progress as the reality of that progress itself.

De l'Esprit des lois had been published only two years earlier, and Turgot's debt to Montesquieu's sociological approach to history was, as he himself admitted, considerable. Yet the differences between their attitudes are probably more significant than the similarities. Montesquieu's approach to human society, in *De l'Esprit des lois* at any rate, was a fundamentally static one. The dimension of time played no part in his work. Wise legislation, he argued in effect, working within the bounds imposed by geography and climate, should aim above all at the creation of a stable society.

Turgot, on the other hand, saw things in essentially dynamic terms. He was unwilling to accept Montesquieu's determinism, and insisted instead on the reality of human freedom, especially the freedom of the genius (in whom he strongly believed) to discover, create and transform. The scientist, the artist, the inventor, were all constantly contributing to the development of civilisation, and this development was the essential subject-matter of history. Of course, Turgot was not so naïve as to deny that there could be setbacks to this process, or to assert that it took place at a uniform rate in each, or all, of its different spheres. Yet because he was looking at various forms of activity (at *les progrès*, rather than *le progrès*), he felt that he could affirm, in some sense, the continuity of progress. In historical times, at any rate, it had never been halted. Turgot shared the current prejudice against the Middle Ages, yet he asserted that even then 'facts were being gathered in the darkness of these ignorant times, and the sciences, whose progress was none the less real for being hidden, were one day to reappear, reinforced by these new riches'.

This claim could hardly be fully substantiated within the framework of two short *Discours*, and to affirm it was something in the nature of an act of faith. Turgot's second main argument, however, seemed more immediately acceptable. If progress could have been halted in the past by natural catastrophes, barbarian invasions, or ignorant tyrants, this was no longer possible. Civilisation had become sufficiently widespread to ensure that if knowledge were obliterated in one country (or even in several), the torch would be taken up elsewhere. If progress was not orginally inevitable, it had now become so.

Turgot's confident affirmations leave many problems behind them. What was the starting-point of progress, and what was the motive force which kept it in being? What was progress itself: was it the accumulation of knowledge in the hands of the wise, or was it the dissemination of this knowledge in ever-widening circles of society? How far was it to be thought of in cultural terms, and how far was its content social and political?

To some of these questions Turgot probably had an answer, though it is not made explicit in the *Discours* themselves. A convinced sensationalist, he probably rooted his idea of the origin of progress in the interaction of man and his environment. His belief in genius (though this was not easy to reconcile with sensationalism) provided an explanation of how the forward leaps were accomplished, Nevertheless, much remained unexplained. Probably Turgot never worked out an explanation, for Christian teleology and materialist determinism were inextricably intertwined in his thought, and it was to the former that he gave his conscious allegiance.

The *Discours* passed unnoticed, and Turgot himself, though he was to make some important philosophical contributions to the *Encyclopédie*, never really worked out his philosophy of history. The task was left to one of his disciples. Yet the marquis de Condorcet, much as he admired Turgot, was to transform the theory of progress into something very different and far more coherent.

Condorcet may be regarded as the last of the *philosophes*. It may be argued that he owes this dignified title to the vigilance of the *sans-culottes* who arrested him when he was trying to escape from Robespierre's reign of terror. Had he not died (very possibly by his own hand) in captivity, he might have survived to become an elder statesman of the Empire and to be classed among the *idéologues* of the early nineteenth century. As things are, the work he wrote when he was in hiding, and which was only published in 1795, after the Thermidorian reaction, has become the supreme symbol of 'Enlightenment' thought. How the symbol is interpreted is a matter of choice. One can, if one wishes, admire the heroic spirit which could proclaim the reality and inevitability of progress after the September massacres and in the very shadow of the guillotine. One may equally well conclude that History itself (this particular capital letter owes much to Condorcet) had carefully staged this particular drama in order to demonstrate the absurdity of 'Enlightenment' optimism.

Avoiding such speculations, let us look at the *Esquisse d'un tableau historique des progrès de l'esprit humain*. Condorcet takes over the two most important arguments of Turgot's *Discours*: progress in the past is an observable historical fact, and the continuation of that progress is now guaranteed, since civilisation has become too widespread to be destroyed. Yet he offers a very different explanation of the way in which progress actually takes place, and he answers many of the questions which Turgot had left untouched.

To begin with, he links the idea of progress with the sensationalist view of human nature in a far more explicit way than did his predecessor. Whilst Turgot believed that man was the creature of his environment, he had tended to attribute the actual steps in human progress to the individual initiative of the 'genius'. The concept of genius does not disappear in Condorcet's work, but it becomes much less dominant. In his discussion of the early stages of human history, he follows in the footsteps of the Rousseau of the *Discours sur l'inégalité*, emphasising the extent to which the pressure of material circumstances forces man, in the interests of self-preservation, to change his way of life. There is a significant element of economic determinism in his thought. Yet, as he traces the development of man through the nine epochs into which he divides past history, he places increasing stress on conscious activity. At times, he seems to hint at Toynbee's theory of challenge and response, though he himself expresses it rather as a continuous search for utility. Men grow in knowledge and power through their efforts to solve concrete problems. They do so, moreover, collectively, for though new discoveries are the work of outstanding individuals, they only become part of the fabric of civilisation when their usefulness is seen by society as a whole.

For Turgot, there was no conflict between religion and progress. For the anti-clerical Condorcet, however, such a conflict became a central theme of history; superstition and priestly intolerance were the main enemies with which civilisation had had to contend throughout the ages. And as Condorcet was an atheist as well as an anti-clerical, there could be no question of a divine purpose behind historical development; teleology seemed to be ruled out. Indeed, it was ruled out in the form in which a Bossuet, or a Turgot even, had conceived of it. It might be more accurate, however, to say that it was incorporated into History itself. Progress became part of the historical process, not by supernatural fiat but by the very nature of things. Condorcet was the first to secularise Pope's deistic affirmation that partial evils constituted universal good. He had not. it is true, developed a theory of historical dialectic in the sort of way Marx was later to do. Yet the way in which he was working towards such a theory is indicated by the many examples he gives of 'History's' ability to produce 'good' from 'evil'. The introduction of cannon and gunpowder, for example, had provided the human race with a new means of destroying itself, yet it had contributed to progress by undermining the power of the feudal knight on horseback, by reducing the possibility of barbarian conquests of civilised peoples and in other ways. Purpose seemed to have been 'built in' to history itself.

If the *Esquisse* contained a sort of secularised teleology, it contained, even more obviously, a secularised eschatology: a vision of a future paradise. During the ninth epoch, which began, according to Condorcet, with Descartes, knowledge had at last become scientific in character, and man had achieved an awareness of his historical destiny. The culmination of this process had been the French Revolution itself, which Condorcet, like many contemporaries, saw as the great turning-point in human affairs. The tenth epoch lay in the future, but it was not difficult to calculate what the future held in store. Once feudal tyranny and priestcraft had been abolished, once liberty and the principles of utilitarianism had been consciously established on a scientific basis, then the way was open for the creation of a new heaven on earth.

Yet if Condorcet's idea of progress contained these apocalyptic overtones, it was nevertheless rooted in the scientific and philosophical principles of the age. Above all, it reflected the new political concepts, foreshadowed in Rousseau or in the American Declaration of Independence, but given their fullest experession in the Revolution. In the *Esquisse*, the idea of progress became linked with that of democracy; the dissemination of knowledge was shown to be more important than its acquisition by a privileged few, and the dissemination of power had to go hand in hand with it. In varying degrees, most of the *philosophes* had subscribed to the so-called double doctrine. 'Not in front of the servants' had been their motto. Truth was for the élite, the geniuses, the *philosophes*; so too was power. The majority might be allowed to cling to their superstitions, or they might be provided with new ones; but in any case they were to be conditioned, led and ruled (however benevolently) by the enlightened minority. In affirming, instead, the fundamental principle of human equality, Condorcet may be said to have set the crown on the Enlightenment.

It is, however, also possible to argue that he and some of his predecessors had so transformed the pattern of human thought that the links between their world and that of Bayle and Fontenelle had almost ceased to exist. I began this book by asserting that the Enlightenment was a remarkably coherent phenomenon. I wish to end it by looking, very briefly, at the other side of the picture.

Dividing lines between historical epochs can never be more than useful approximations, and we may feel, like Buffon did about Linnaeus, that an obsession with pigeon-holes often does more harm than good. Condorcet drew his lines approximately where I have done: through Descartes and the French Revolution. Yet if he had lived to witness the Bourbon Restoration and the rise of Romanticism, he might have had second thoughts. He might have found that the generation of 1780 had more in common with Comte or Marx than with Descartes, or even Condillac, and that Rousseau's *La Nouvelle Héloïse* was much closer to Stendhal's *Le Rouge et le noir* than to Fénelon's *Télémaque*. Diderot, I suspect, would be more at home with Saint-Simon, or even Darwin, than with Newton. There is, in

160

short, in the history of ideas, a powerful case for drawing a line through the middle of the eighteenth century rather than through the politically significant date of 1789. In the first half of the century, one may argue, men were searching for stability. They sought it in politics, after a century of war and civil strife; Locke proclaimed the ideal of a 'mixed' government based on respect for property and the liberties of the individual; Fénelon, and the French 'neo-feudalists', looked for refuge from recent disasters in an idealised past of stratified, but secure, social relationships; Montesquieu followed both Locke and Fénelon, but also wanted to bring man into conscious harmony with the forces that shaped his destiny. They sought it, too, in religion, science and philosophy, three fields which they never clearly separated; toleration offered the hope of an end to the ceaseless strife of Protestant and Catholic, Jansenist and Jesuit, Anglican and Presbyterian; deism and 'reasonable Christianity' provided a more positive focus for unity; the Newtonian universe, ordered, unchanging, the supreme creation of the divine artificer, gave them a celestial model for what they hoped to achieve on earth. Moderation, culture, good taste, science, benevolence – the qualities and pursuits admired by Steele, Addison or Shaftesbury, by Saint-Pierre, Voltaire, or Marivaux – seemed to them the passports to civilised life.

By the middle of the century, a change was becoming apparent. For Turgot, man's aim was progress, not stability. The political radicals, Helvétius, d'Holbach, Rousseau, though they did not adhere to a theory of progress and were far from united in their beliefs, were all putting forward more dynamic views of society, with the emphasis on reform, on development, on education, on leadership. The deist compromise still had its adherents, but from the time of La Mettrie onwards it was being superseded by a more assertive and uncompromising atheism. The Newtonian world-view, though by no means abandoned, was giving place to one rooted in the biological sciences, one which emphasised evolution and transformation rather than order. Enthusiasm, a word

161

which in the earlier part of the century had conjured up visions of religious fanaticism, became not merely respectable but also essential to anyone who aspired to the dignity of being called *une âme sensible*. The concept of genius, basically alien to sensationalism, invaded the thought even of those who remained sensationalists.

To attempt to choose between this view of eighteenth-century French thought and the one expressed in my opening chapter would, I believe, be a mistake. They contradict each other, but they are both 'true' like the opposing arguments in a Diderot dialogue. The mid-century break is a significant one, but it would be arbitrary to affirm that either half of the age constituted the 'real' Enlightenment. Unity and diversity are logically difficult to reconcile, but only by accepting this dialectical complexity of the development of thought can be phenomenon like 'the Enlightenment' be understood.

Appendix

Bibliographical Sketch

It would obviously be impossible, within the scope of this book, to give any sort of fully representative bibliography of the many authors and subjects on which I have touched. Much detailed information may be found in *A Critical Bibliography of French Literature: The Eighteenth Century*, edited by G. R. Havens and D. F. Bond (1951) and in its *Supplement*, edited by R. A. Brooks (1968). These volumes deal extensively with the history of ideas as well as with 'literature' in the narrower sense. They are, however, less helpful on political and social history. Here, the two volumes of *Clio. Le XVIIIe siècle*, edited by E. Préclin and V. L. Tapié (1952), are invaluable. Most readers will find that the excellent bibliographical essay in P. Gay's *The Enlightenment: An Interpretation. The Rise of Modern Paganism* (1966) contains all they require, and there are useful shorter lists in two Penguin Books: the first volume of A. Cobban's *A History of Modern France* (1957), and N. Hampson's *The Enlightenment* (1968).

Here, I propose to be very selective. I shall restrict myself to books on the eighteenth century; I shall show a bias towards recent works and towards those available in English; lastly I shall emphasise those which raise problems rather than those which give information.

Chapter 1

The classic study is Ernst Cassirer's *The Philosophy of the Enlightenment* (originally 1932; English translation, 1951). Its penetrating analysis of the thought of the age will not easily be surpassed. It is, however, the sort of book which demands a good deal of prior knowledge from the reader. It has also a certain pro-German orientation, understandably enough, since Cassirer sees the European Enlightenment as culminating in Kant. This is an eminently tenable view for a philosopher, but it leads Cassirer to neglect some of the social aspects of the Enlightenment, particularly as far as France is concerned.

Paul Hazard goes less deeply into the philosophy of the Enlightenment, but views the movement as a whole in a wider perspective. His two books, *La Crise de la conscience européenne* (1935) and *La Pensée européenne au XVIIIe siècle* (1948) are both available in Penguin translations. The first, which deals with the period 1680–1715, is highly readable (though not without a certain French *préciosité*) and well informed. One may question its assertion that this period constituted *the* crisis in European thought, but it was certainly *a* crisis, and Hazard is not a dogmatic writer. His second book does not have quite the same impact, but is remarkably wide in its range.

Among more recent works, J. F. Lively's *The Enlightenment* (1966) contains a useful selection of texts, and René Pomeau's *L'Europe des lumières* (1966) brings to life the cosmopolitan spirit of the age. Norman Hampson's *The Enlightenment* (Penguin Books, 1968), is now the best short account available in English, well constructed and well informed. But the most weighty contribution of recent years is that contained in the two volumes (1966 and 1969) of Peter Gay's *The Enlightenment: An Interpretation*. An immensely wide knowledge, an attractive style and penetrating insight are all found here. Gay stresses, particularly in his first volume, the debt which the Enlightenment owed to Antiquity, and it is possible to argue that this theme is given a little more prominence than it deserves. Nevertheless, his work is likely to remain, for a long time, the most reliable authority on the Enlightenment as a whole.

To turn to works dealing purely with the French

Enlightenment, John Lough's *Introduction to Eighteenth-century France* is balanced and broadly based, whilst the first volume of Maxime Leroy's *Histoire des idées sociales en France* (1946) is useful on political thought. The most complete work of research is Daniel Mornet's *Les Origines intellectuelles de la Révolution française* (1933), a mine of information, though less satisfactory from the point of view of understanding. Mornet's shorter work, *La Pensée française au dix-huitième siècle* (1926), is clear, if unadventurous. R. J. White's *The Anti-Philosophers* (1970) restricts itself mainly to the Encyclopedists, and is most successful in bringing them to life as individuals, though it perhaps undervalues them as philosophical thinkers.

The interpretation of the Enlightenment can still arouse fairly passionate controversy. I shall ignore its overt enemies, and mention three works which have been held to attack it from within. C. L. Becker's *The Heavenly City of the Eighteenth-century Philosophers* (1932) is a superb piece of writing, but its main contention, that the *philosophes* built a secularised version of the Christian 'city of God', overemphasises what is certainly a significant aspect of their thinking. Becker is adept at constructing an 'Aunt Sally' *philosophe*, compounded from innumerable real ones, and then proceeding to knock him down. Not surprisingly, there have been many replies, one of the best being that by Peter Gay in his *The Party of Humanity* (1954), a volume which contains many other valuable essays. A very different attack on the Enlightenment has been discerned in J. L. Talmon's *The Origins of Totalitarian Democracy* (1952). Talmon deals mainly with the thought of the Revolutionary period, but also with some of the later *philosophes*. Though he does not contend that the Enlightenment in general is a distant ancestor of Hitler and Stalin, he does suggest that this is the case with aspects of the thought of Helvétius, d'Holbach, Rousseau and others. Once again admirers of the Enlightenment have been quick to reply (like many *philosophes* themselves, we are, perhaps, a thin-skinned lot). Alfred Cobban's *In Search of Humanity*

(1960) contains one of the best-argued defences of Enlightenment liberalism.

A much more weighty argument is to be found in two volumes by L. G. Crocker: *An Age of Crisis: Man and World in Eighteenth Century Thought* (1959) and *Nature and Culture: Ethical Thought in the French Enlightenment* (1963). These volumes, particularly the latter, constitute a major work of scholarship, and contain some of the best appreciations I know of many aspects of Enlightenment thought. However, they also contain an implicit condemnation of this thought in the emphasis they place on the link between Enlightenment philosophy and the theory (and practice) of the marquis de Sade. This emphasis seems to me, as to many others, exaggerated. I think it would be truer to say that Sadism slips through a loophole than that it is connected by a link.

Chapter 2

Two important background books on seventeenth-century philosophy (I shall not list more) are Emile Bréhier's *Histoire de la philosophie* (vol. II, 1929) and J. H. Randall's *The Career of Philosophy* (vol. I, 1965). The latter, which covers the period from the Middle Ages to the Enlightenment, laying particular emphasis on the philosophy of science, is a most impressive work. Unfortunately, Randall is somewhat less at home in the French Enlightenment than in most areas of this vast field.

On Bayle, there is a useful general study in English by Howard Robinson entitled *Bayle the Sceptic* (1931). The most important recent work is that of Elizabeth Labrousse, *Pierre Bayle* (2 vols, 1963–4). H. T. Mason's *Pierre Bayle and Voltaire* (1963) and W. H. Barber's *Leibniz in France* (1955) are both helpful. The best treatment of Fontenelle is to be found in J. R. Carré's *La Philosophie de Fontenelle ou Le Sourire de la raison* (1932), though Robert Shackleton's edition of the *Entretiens sur la pluralité des mondes* and the *Digression sur les anciens et les modernes* (1955) has much to add.

Alexander Koyré's *Newtonian Studies* (1965) contains some illuminating articles on Newton's significance. The best account of his early influence in France is to be found in Pierre Brunet's *L'Introduction des théories de Newton en France au XVIIIe siècle* (1931). Gerd Buchdahl's *The Image of Newton and Locke in the Age of Reason* (1961) is brief, but useful, and Gabriel Bonno's *La Culture et la civilisation britanniques devant l'opinion française de la paix d'Utrecht aux 'Lettres philosophiques'* (1948) covers the subject well.

Chapter 3

Alfred Cobban's *A History of Modern France* (Penguin Books, 1957) and C. B. A. Behrens' *The Ancien Régime* (1967) provide an excellent historical background to this and subsequent chapters. More detailed are the two volumes of Philippe Sagnac's *La Formation de la société française moderne* (1945 and 1946). Antoine Adam's *Le Mouvement philosophique dans la première moitié du XVIIIe siècle* (1967) is particularly good on the social background to the struggles of the early *philosophes*, as is J. S. Spink's *French Free Thought from Gassendi to Voltaire* (1960) on their intellectual origins. The influence of Spinoza, important throughout the century, is the subject of Paul Vernière's masterly two-volume *Spinoza et la pensée française avant la Révolution* (1954), and the general dissemination of early 'philosophic' ideas is studied in I. O. Wade's *The Clandestine Organisation and Diffusion of Philosophic ideas in France from 1700 to 1750* (1938). Geoffrey Atkinson's *The Extraordinary Voyage in French Literature from 1700 to 1722* covers this important subject very thoroughly.

Vauban has been rather neglected recently, but there is a thorough study of his life and writings by Rochas d'Aiglun, *Vauban, sa famille et ses écrits...* (2 vols, 1910) and a good edition of the *Dîme royale* by E. Coornaert (1933). On Fénelon, Élie Carcassonne's

Fénelon; l'homme et l'oeuvre (1946) is sound, and Albert Chérel's *Fénelon au XVIIIe siècle en France; son prestige, son influence* (1917) is likewise valuable.

Chapter 4

Kingsley Martin's *French Liberal Thought in the Eighteenth Century* (1929) covers the whole field from Bayle to Condorcet, with special emphasis on political thought. It is beginning to date now in many details, but remains a most valuable conspectus of the age. Henri Sée's brief *La France économique et sociale au XVIIIe siècle* (1925) also shows signs of age, but is very clear. An important recent study is F. L. Ford's *Robe and Sword: The Regrouping of the French Aristocracy after Louis XIV* (1953) which shows how the two branches of the nobility came together to form a united opposition led by the *Parlements*. E. G. Barber's *The Bourgeoisie in 18th Century France* (1955), though less solid, forms a useful complement.

Saint-Pierre is well served by Joseph Drouet's *L'abbé de Saint-Pierre, l'homme et l'œuvre* (1912) and M. L. Perkins' *The Moral and Political Philosophy of the abbé de Saint-Pierre* (1959), though neither book fully penetrates the complexity of this fascinating writer. Renée Simon's *Henry de Boulainviller [sic]; historien, politique, philosophe, astrologue* (1939) is one of those exhaustive and utterly competent French theses which, by their very completeness, fail to produce an impact; but there is nothing better. The same may be said of Alfred Lombard's *L'abbé Du Bos; un initiateur de la pensée moderne* (1913).

On Voltaire, a vast amount has been written. Among the good short studies are those by Gustave Lanson (revised edn, 1965), H. N. Brailsford (1935), R. Naves (1942) and V. W. Topazio (1967). The latest and most accurate biography is that by Th. Besterman (1969). René Pomeau's *La Religion de Voltaire* (1956) is outstanding, and only slightly less so is Peter Gay's *Voltaire's Politics* (1959). Norman Torrey's *The Spirit of Voltaire* (1938) is a most sympathetic study. The *Let-*

168

tres philosophiques themselves have been the subject of a classic 'critical edition' by Lanson (revised, 1964). I shall have occasion to return to other specific aspects of Voltaire.

Montesquieu, too, does not lack interpreters. Robert Shackleton's *Montesquieu: A Critical Biography* (1961) is a work of great authority, though more concerned with the origins of Montesquieu's thought than with its significance. Louis Althusser's *Montesquieu; la politique et l'histoire* (1959), on the other hand, is a brief but penetrating analysis of what Montesquieu 'meant' to his own and subsequent generations. Older works are still valuable, particularly Henri Barckhausen's *Montesquieu, ses idées et ses œuvres d'après les papiers de La Brède* (1907), Élie Carcassonne's *Montesquieu et le problème de la constitution française au XVIIIe siècle* (1927) and Joseph Dedieu's *Montesquieu* (1913). There is an excellent edition of the *Lettres persanes* by Paul Vernière (1960) and of *De l'Esprit des lois* by Jean Brèthe de La Gressaye (1950-8).

Chapter 5

Here, I shall avoid details, and mention just four works, all of major importance. A. O. Lovejoy's *The Great Chain of Being* (1936) studies the history of this concept from Plato to the Romantics, and although some modern historians of ideas look askance at such an approach, his work is a superb combination of erudition, insight and style. J. Ehrard's *L'Idée de la Nature en France dans la première moitié de XVIIIe siècle* (2 vols, 1963) contains an exhaustive analysis of the most complex concept of the age. 'Happiness', however, is only a shade less complex, and perhaps even more indefinable. R. Mauzi's *L'Idée du bonheur au XVIIIe siècle* (1960) covers its many aspects with great thoroughness. Finally, Jacques Roger's *Les sciences de la vie dans la pensée française du XVIIIe siècle* (1963) supersedes previous studies and is the best authority on many questions discussed here and in the next chapter.

Chapter 6

Georges Le Roy's edition of the *Œuvres philosophiques de Condillac* (3 vols, 1947–51) is good; otherwise Condillac has been somewhat neglected by editors. Roger Lefèvre's *Condillac, ou la joie de vivre* (1966) is clear, but I. F. Knight's *The Geometric Spirit. The Abbé de Condillac and the French Enlightenment* (1968) is the best available study, perceptive and well written. La Mettrie has also been neglected, though Aram Vartanian's edition of *L'Homme machine* has a long and excellent introduction. L. C. Rosenfield's *From Beast-machine to Man-machine: Animal Soul in French Letters from Descartes to La Mettrie* (1941) is also useful.

Colm Kiernan's *Science and the Enlightenment in Eighteenth-century France* (1968) somewhat overstates a good case. Maupertuis is well served by Pierre Brunet's study (2 vols, 1929). *On Voltaire, Historian* there is my own book (1957).

Diderot is perhaps the most 'alive' of all the *philosophes* at the moment. There are excellent Garnier editions of his *Œuvres philosophiques* (1956), *Œuvres esthétiques* (1959) and *Œuvres politiques* (1963) all by Paul Vernière, and of individual works by Niklaus, Dieckmann, Seznec and others. L. W. Tancock has provided a Penguin translation of *Le Neveu de Rameau* and *Le Rêve de d'Alembert* (1966). Among general studies, L. G. Crocker's *The Embattled Philosopher* (1954). A. M. Wilson's *Diderot: the Testing Years, 1713–1759* (1957) and Jean Thomas's *L'Humanisme de Diderot* (1932) are all valuable. Daniel Mornet's *Diderot* (1941) is clear but not penetrating; Henri Lefebvre's *Diderot* (1949) is penetrating, but rather dogmatically Marxist. Aram Vartanian's *Diderot and Descartes: a Study of Scientific Naturalism in the Enlightenment* (1953) is impressive.

Chapter 7

R. R. Palmer's *The Age of the Democratic Revolution* (2 vols, 1959 and 1964) is a most valuable historical study of this later period. On the *Encyclopédie*, there is a useful introductory study by Pierre Grosclaude: *Un audacieux Message: L'Encyclopédie* (1951). René Hubert's *Les Sciences sociales dans l'Encyclopédie* (1923) remains important. Two most thorough recent studies, however, have transformed many aspects of the interpretation of the work: Jacques Proust's *Diderot et l'Encyclopédie* (1962) has emphasised the importance of the work for the development of Diderot's own thought and provided a great deal of new information about contributors and subscribers. John Lough's *Essays on the Encyclopédie of Diderot and D'Alembert* (1968) – an excellent book, though not for popular consumption – has ably continued the latter task in particular. Pierre Grosclaude's *Malesherbes, témoin et interprète de son temps* (1961) is a full-length study of the *Encyclopédie*'s protector.

There is a useful edition of selections from Helvétius' *De l'Esprit* by Guy Besse (1959) and a thorough study of the events surrounding its publication in D. W. Smith's *Helvétius: A Study in Persecution* (1965). Elie Halévy's *The Growth of Philosophic Radicalism* (1934) is excellent on the history of utilitarianism. The best book on d'Holbach is that by Pierre Naville (1943). Ronald Grimsley's *Jean d'Alembert* (1963) is very thorough.

For a brief analysis of Voltaire's attitude at the time of *Candide*, see my edition of the *conte* (1968). The best study of the Calas affair itself is D. D. Bien's *The Calas Affair* (1960). Edna Nixon's *Voltaire and the Calas Case* (1961) is less penetrating, but very readable. Jane Ceitac's *Voltaire et l'affaire des natifs* (1956) carefully examines his relationship with the Genevan dissidents, and Renéè Waldinger's *Voltaire and Reform* (1959) outlines the various aspects of his programme and links it with popular demands at the time of the French Revolution. See also the works on Voltaire listed under Chapter Four.

Douglas Dakin's *Turgot and the Ancien Régime in France* (1939) is authoritative on his career as a whole, though not particularly concerned with his philosophy. The best treatment of his theory of progress is to be found in F. E. Manuel's *The Prophets of Paris* (1962), which is equally excellent on Condorcet. Condorcet's *Sketch* is now available in an English translation by June Barraclough (1955). The standard French edition is by O. H. Prior (1933).

The importance of the idea of progress in the Enlightenment has naturally been stressed by students of that idea itself, such as J. B. Bury (*The Idea of Progress*, 1920). In a wide-ranging, though not very deep book, *Historical Pessimism in the French Enlightenment*, Henry Vyverberg has stressed the other side of the coin (1958). In an illuminating article in vol. LVIII of the *Studies on Voltaire and the Eighteenth Century* (1967), Norman Suckling distinguishes between the different senses of 'progress', and suggests further that those who used the word most frequently were not the ones who contributed most to progress itself. The same article is germane to my concluding remarks, for Suckling tends to see. in the work of the writers of the second half of the century, something of a betrayal of the real spirit of the Enlightenment. I would not go quite all the way with him here, but his article, and Roland Mortier's 'Unité ou scission du siècle des lumières?' (*Studies on Voltaire*, vol. XXVI, 1963) constitute two of the most important contributions to a continuing debate.

With rare exceptions, I have deliberately excluded articles from this bibliography. I cannot end, however, without mentioning the most important source of them. The *Studies on Voltaire and the Eighteenth Century*, edited by Theodore Besterman, have become, since the first volume appeared in 1955, the main vehicle for the dissemination of new ideas on eighteenth-century thought and literature; over seventy volumes have so far appeared. *Diderot Studies*, edited by O. E. Fellows and others, though more modest in scope, is also most valuable.

Name Index

Alembert, Jean le Rond d', 19, 42, 56, 99, 107, 130, 139–41, 143, 144, 145, 154, 171
Argenson, René-Louis Voyer, marquis d', 64, 67, 135, 149

Bacon, Francis, 14, 140, 154
Bayle, Pierre, 18, 22, 34–8, 39, 40, 48, 49, 90, 115, 122, 150, 160, 166
Beccaria, Cesare, 23, 153
Berkeley, George, 9, 105, 106
Bertrand, Élie, 93, 113
Biran, Maine de, 102, 107
Boerhaave, Hermann, 21
Boisguillebert, Pierre de, 55
Bolingbroke, Henry St John, 23, 24, 69
Bossuet, Jacques-Bénigne, 11–12, 31, 47, 56, 117, 159
Boulainvilliers, Henri de, 59, 64–7, 117, 168
Buffon, Georges-Louis Leclerc de, 10, 96, 105, 110, 112, 113, 134, 139, 140, 160

Calas, Jean, 134, 152, 171
Chaumeix, Abraham, 148, 149
Choiseul, Étienne-François, duc de, 149, 153
Clarke, Samuel, 24
Colbert, Jean-Baptiste, 45, 47, 55
Collins, Anthony, 24
Condillac, Étienne-Bonnot de, 9, 43, 99–107, 110, 111, 113, 130, 136, 140, 142, 160, 170
Condorcet, Marie-Jean-Antoine-Nicolas, marquis de, 87, 99, 157–9, 160, 172

Derham, William, 92–3
Descartes, René, 9, 11, 13–17 passim, 22, 23, 27–43 passim, 92, 94, 100, 108, 109, 110, 123, 140, 154, 160

Diderot, Denis, 9, 10, 19, 23, 87, 88, 91, 94, 96, 97, 99, 105, 107, 110, 111, 113, 115, 118, 119–32, 134, 139–46 passim, 154, 160, 170
Dubois, Guillaume, cardinal, 60–2
Dubos, Jean-Baptiste, 67–8, 75, 168

Fénelon, François de Salignac de la Mothe-, 49, 51, 55–9, 62, 160, 167–8
Fleury, André-Hercule, cardinal de, 66, 135
Fontenelle, Bernard le Bovier de, 32, 33, 34, 38–42, 87, 154, 166
Frederick II (of Prussia), 23, 108, 135, 147, 148

Galileo, 11, 14
Gassendi, Pierre, 31, 35, 167
Gibbon, Edward, 23, 24, 34, 117
Grimm, Friedrich Melchior, 76

Helvétius, Claude-Adrien, 97, 99, 107, 134, 136–7, 143–4, 160, 165, 171
Hobbes, Thomas, 73, 77, 78, 107
Holbach, Paul Henri Thiry, baron d', 7, 23, 68, 91, 94, 111, 134, 137, 142, 143, 151, 160, 165, 171
Hume, David, 9, 13, 23, 25, 33

Jurieu, Pierre, 38, 48

Kant, Immanuel, 9, 18, 63, 164

La Bruyère, Jean de, 49–50, 54, 73
La Mettrie, Julien Offroy de, 32, 91, 97, 107–12, 131, 160, 170

Subject Index

absolutism and despotism, 46–7, 51, 52, 67, 68, 71, 74, 79, 80, 81, 82, 153
anthropology, 88, 89, 114, 117
anti-clericalism 44, 52, 54, 96–7, 137, 147–52, 158–9
aristocracy, its role in the French Enlightenment, 20, 45, 50, 52, 53, 54, 58, 59, 63–7
astronomy, 11, 15, 20, 30, 36, 39, 41, 92, 95, 124
atheism, 16, 32, 33, 38, 122–4, 126–7, 130, 151, 161
authority, 13–14, 30, 36, 40, 52

biology, 109–15, 124, 150–1, 160, 169
bourgeoisie, its role in the French Enlightenment, 19, 20, 21, 24, 44–5, 68–72

Catholicism, 11, 12, 14, 34, 37, 46, 49, 54, 58, 122–4

deism, 14, 33, 35, 37, 38, 52, 59, 69, 74, 93, 120, 122–4, 147–51, 161
democracy, 10, 12, 16, 63–4, 80–1, 83–4, 86, 159–60
despotism, *see* absolutism
determinism, 75, 84–5, 87, 105, 124, 128–9, 156

economics, 55–6, 61, 63, 72, 133
Encyclopédie, 19, 20, 128, 134, 138–46, 150, 157, 171
Enlightenment: definition of, 9 ff.; cosmopolitanism of, 21–3; in England, 24; in Scotland, 24–5, 76, 120; in Spain, 25–6
epistemology, 16, 101–7, 125
evolution, 12, 95–6, 111–15, 117, 127, 130–1, 160

'extraordinary voyages', 51–2, 73, 167
French Revolution (the), 7, 53, 70, 137, 159–60

genius, 137, 144, 157, 158, 162
geology (and palaeontology), 10, 93–4, 111, 113–15
'Great Chain of Being' (the), 94–6, 112, 169

hedonism, 91, 97–8, 169
history and historiography, 13, 31, 35, 40, 64–8, 75, 115–18, 155–9, 172

idealism, 16, 32, 105, 106
imagination, 33, 40, 102, 105, 110, 121
innate ideas, 16, 35, 42, 101, 102, 103, 109
instinct, 78, 88, 103

Jansenism, 31, 42, 58, 60, 61, 120, 134

language, 103–4, 109

materialism, 29–32, 91, 104, 105, 107–10, 119, 123, 125–7, 143–4
mathematics, 15, 29, 41
moral philosophy, 7, 36, 40, 87–8, 121–2, 126, 128–9, 131

natural law, 46, 77–8, 85, 109
nature and natural goodness, 12, 88–98, 124, 128–9, 169

palaeontology, *see* geology
Parlements, 45, 53, 60, 61, 66–9, 134, 136, 142, 144, 151–3
political theory, 12, 16–17, 45–8, 52, 57–8, 62–86, 135, 152–3
polysynody, 62–4, 74

175